Carrying on in Key Stage 1

Providing continuity in purposeful play and exploration

Role Play

Ros Bayley, Lynn Broadbent, Sally Featherstone

Reprinted 2009
Published 2008 by A&C Black Publishers Limited
36 Soho Square, London W1D 3QY
www.acblack.com

ISBN 978-1-906029-43-2

First published 2008 by Featherstone Education Limited

Text © Ros Bayley, Lyn Broadbent, Sally Featherstone 2008
Illustrations © Kerry Ingham 2008
Photographs © Lynn Broadbent, Ros Bayley,
Sally Featherstone, Sarah Featherstone 2008

A CIP record for this publication is available from the British Library.

Printed in Malta by Gutenberg Press Ltd

This book is produced using paper that is made from wood grown in
managed, sustainable forests. It is natural, renewable and recyclable.
The logging and manufacturing processes conform to the environmental
regulations of the country of origin.

To see our full range of titles

visit www.acblack.com

Contents

Introduction

This series of books is intended to support the continuing growth and development of independent learning and practical activities, which are key features of the Early Years Foundation Stage.

Children in Key Stage One need and deserve the chance to **build on the best of practice in the Early Years Foundation Stage**, which carefully balances adult directed tasks with learning that children initiate and develop themselves, often in the company of responsive adults. These activities, which include sand and water play, construction, role play, independent mark making and writing, creative work, dance and movement, and outdoor play, are some of the activities children value most and miss most in Years One and Two.

> Parent: 'What's it like in Year 1?'
>
> Child: 'There en't no sand and the work's too 'ard.'

This quote from a Year 1 boy echoes the feelings of many children who need to continue the learning styles and situations offered in Reception classes. However, many teachers in Key Stage One feel intense pressure to concentrate on activities that require recording and increasing levels of direction by adults. Why is this, and is it right for teachers to feel so pressured?

One thing we know from research is that **practical activity and independent learning are essential for brain growth** and reinforcement of growing abilities throughout childhood, at least till the onset of puberty, and for many children this is a lifelong need. We also know that the embedding of learning and the transformation of this into real understanding takes time and practice. Skills need to be reinforced by revisiting them in many different contexts in child initiated learning, and practical challenges, and practical tasks in real life situations will be far more effective than rote learning, worksheets or adult direction.

> 'I hear and I forget,
>
> I see and I remember,
>
> I do and I understand.'
>
> Ancient Chinese Proverb

EVERY CHILD MATTERS
The five outcomes:
Enjoy and achieve
Stay safe
Be healthy
Make a positive contribution
Achieve economic well-being

It is also clear from brain research that **many boys (and some girls) are just not ready by the end of Reception to embark on a formal curriculum** which involves a lot of sitting down, listening and writing. Their bodies and their brains still need action, challenge and freedom to explore materials and resources in freedom.

But this does not mean that challenge should be absent from such activity! The brain feeds on challenge and novelty, so teachers and other adults working in Key Stage One need to structure the experiences, so they build on existing skills and previous activities, while presenting new opportunities to explore familiar materials in new and exciting ways. Such challenges and activities can:

- be led by the Programme of Study for Key Stage One;
- focus on thinking skills and personal capabilities;
- relate to real world situations and stimuli;
- help children to achieve the five outcomes for Every Child Matters.

In **Carrying on in Key Stage 1**, we aim to give you the rationale, the process and the confidence to continue a practical, child centred curriculum which also helps you as teachers to recognise the requirements of the **statutory curriculum for Key Stage One**. Each book in the series follows the same format, and addresses objectives from many areas of the National Curriculum. Of course, when children work on practical challenges, curriculum elements become intertwined, and many will be going on simultaneously.

The Role of the Adult

Of course, even during child initiated learning, **the role of the adult is crucial**. Sensitive adults play many roles as they support, challenge and engage the children in their care. High quality teaching is not easy! If teachers want to expand experiences and enhance learning, they need to be able to stand back, to work alongside, <u>and</u> extend or scaffold the children's learning by offering provocations and challenges to their thinking and activity. The diagram below attempts to describe this complex task, and the way that adults move around the elements in the circle of learning. For ease of reading we have described the elements in the following way, and each double page spread covers all three of the vital roles adults play.

Recognising and building on the practical activities which children have experienced before

This element of the process is vital in scaffolding children's learning so it makes sense to them. Your knowledge of the Foundation Stage curriculum and the way it is organised will be vital in knowing where to start. Teachers and other adults should have first hand knowledge of both the resources and the activities which have been available and how they have been offered in both child initiated and adult led activities. This knowledge should be gained by visiting the Reception classes in action, and by talking to adults and children as they work. Looking at Reception planning will also help.

Understanding the range of adult roles, and the effect different roles have on children's learning

Responsive adults react in different ways to what they see and hear during the day. This knowledge will influence the way they plan for further experiences which meet emerging needs and build on individual interests. The diagram illustrates the complex and interlinking ways in which adults interact with children's learning. Observing, co-playing and extending learning often happen simultaneously, flexibly and sometime unconsciously. It is only when we reflect on our work with children that we realise what a complex and skilled activity is going on.

Offering challenges and provocations

As the adults collect information about the learning, they begin to see how they can help children to extend and scaffold their thinking and learning. The adults offer challenges or provocations which act like grit in an oyster, provoking the children to produce responses and think in new ways about what they know and can do.

Linking the learning with the skills and content of the curriculum

As the children grapple with new concepts and skills, adults can make direct links with curriculum intentions and content. These links can be mapped out across the range of knowledge, skills and understanding contained in the curriculum guidance for Key Stage One. It is also possible to map the development of thinking skills, personal capabilities and concepts which link the taught curriculum with the real world.

The adult as extender of learning
discusses ideas
shares thinking
makes new possibilities evident
instigates new opportunities for learning
extends and builds on learning and interests
supports children in making links in learning
models new skills and techniques

The adult as co-player
shares responsibility with the child
offers suggestions
asks open questions
responds sensitively
models and imitates
plays alongside

The adult as observer
listens attentively
observes carefully
records professionally
interprets skilfully

Looking for the Learning

As children plan, explore, invent, extend, construct, discuss, question and predict in the rich experiences planned and offered, they will communicate what they are learning through speech and actions, as well as through the outcomes of activities. **Assessment for learning** involves adults and children in discussing and analysing what they discover. Reflecting on learning, through discussion with other children and adults, is a key factor in securing skills and abilities, fixing and 'hard wiring' the learning in each child's brain. And, of course, teachers and other adults need to **recognise, confirm and record children's achievements**, both for the self esteem this brings to the children and to fulfil their own duties as educators.

You could find out what children already know and have experienced by:

* talking to them as individuals and in small groups;

* talking to parents and other adults who know them well (teaching assistants are often wonderful sources of information about individual children);

* visiting the Reception classes and looking at spaces, storage and access to resources, including the use of these out of doors;

* providing free access to materials and equipment and watching how children use them when you are not giving any guidance;

* talking as a group or class about what children already know about the materials and those they particularly enjoy using.

Using the curriculum grid to observe, to recognise learning and celebrate achievement

At the end of each section you will find a curriculum grid which covers the whole Programme of Study for Key Stage 1. This is a 'shorthand version' of the full grid included at the end of the book on pages 69-74. A black and white photocopiable version of the grid appears on page 8, so you can make your own copies for planning and particularly for recording observations.

We suggest that as the children work on the provocations and other challenges in this book, adults (teachers and teaching assistants) can use the grid to observe groups of children and record the areas of the curriculum they are covering in their work. The grids can also be used to record what children say and describe in plenary sessions and other discussions.

These observations will enable you to recognise the learning that happens as children explore the materials and engage with the challenging questions you ask and the problems you pose. And of course, as you observe, you will begin to see what needs to happen next; identifying the next steps in learning! This logical and vital stage in the process may identify:

* some children who will be ready for more of the same activity;

* some who need to repeat and reinforce previous stages;

* some who need to relate skills to new contexts, the same activity or skill practiced in a new place or situation;

* some who will want to extend or sustain the current activity in time, space or detail;

* others who will wish to record their work in photos, drawings, models, stories, video etc.

> "Imaginative play gives children opportunities to explore and represent actions, role, relationships, situations, characters from a variety of sources, narratives and stories."
> Bernadette Duffy in 'Supporting Creativity and Imagination in the Early Years'

Critical and Thinking Skills

The grid also identifies the key skills which children need for thinking about and evaluating their work. Many schools now observe and evaluate how well these skills are developing when children work on challenging projects and investigations.

Taking it further

Offering extension activities is a way of scaffolding children's learning, taking the known into the unknown, the familiar into the new, the secure into the challenging. It is the role of the adult to turn their knowledge of the children into worthwhile, long term lines of enquiry and development which will become self-sustaining and last throughout life.

At the end of each section in the book you will find a selection of useful resources, links and other information to help you bring construction to life. You could use these resources by encouraging individuals and groups:

* to **use the Internet** to find images and information;

* to **use ICT equipment** such as cameras, tape recorders, video and dictaphones to record their explorations and experiments;

* to **explore information books** in libraries and other places at home and at school;

* to **make contact by email and letter** with experts, craftsmen, artists, manufacturers, suppliers and other contacts;

* to **make books, films, PowerPoint presentations**;

* to **record their work** in photographs and other media;

* to **respond to stimuli** such as photographs, video, exhibitions and other creative stimuli;

* to **look at the built and natural environment** with curiosity, interest and creativity;

* to **become involved in preserving the natural world**, develop environmental awareness and support recycling;

* to **look at the world of work** and extend their ideas of what they might become and how they might live their lives;

* to **develop a sense of economic awareness** and the world of work in its widest sense;

* to **feel a sense of community** and to explore how they might make a contribution to the school and wider communities in which they live;

* to **work together and develop the ability to think, reason and solve problems** in their learning.

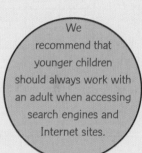

We recommend that younger children should always work with an adult when accessing search engines and Internet sites.

The suggested resources include websites, books, contacts and addresses. There are also some photographs which may inspire young learners as they work on the provocations and challenges suggested.

We hope you will find the ideas in this book useful in stimulating your work with children in Year 1 and Year 2. The ideas, photos and provocations we have included are only a start to your thinking and exploring together, of course you and the children will have many more as you start to expand the work they do in these practical areas, providing a rich curriculum base using familiar and well loved materials.

Ros Bayley, Lynn Broadbent, Sally Featherstone: 2008

Observation of _____ (the activity and resources)

Literacy

	Lit 1 speak	Lit 2 listen	Lit 3 group	Lit 4 drama	Lit 5 word	Lit 6 spell	Lit 7 text1	Lit 8 text2	Lit 9 text3	Lit10 text4	Lit11 sentence	Lit12 presentation
	1.1	2.1	3.1	4.1	5.1	6.1	7.1	8.1	9.1	10.1	11.1	12.1
	1.2	2.2	3.2	4.2	5.2	6.2	7.2	8.2	9.2	10.2	11.2	12.2

Numeracy

	Num 1 U&A	Num 2 count	Num 3 number	Num 4 calculate	Num 5 shape	Num 6 measure	Num 7 data
	1.1	2.1	3.1	4.1	5.1	6.1	7.1
	1.2	2.2	3.2	4.2	5.2	6.2	7.2

Date	
Names	

Science

	SC1 Enquiry			SC2 Life processes					SC3 Materials		SC4 Phys processes		
	Sc1.1	Sc1.2	Sc1.3	Sc2.1	Sc2.2	Sc2.3	Sc2.4	Sc2.5	Sc3.1	Sc3.2	Sc4.1	Sc4.2	Sc4.3
	1.1a	1.2a	1.3a	2.1a	2.2a	2.3a	2.4a	2.5a	3.1a	3.2a	4.1a	4.2a	4.3a
	1.1b	1.2b	1.3b	2.1b	2.2b	2.3b	2.4b	2.5b	3.1b	3.2b	4.1b	4.2b	4.3b
	1.1c	1.2c	1.3c	2.1c	2.2c	2.3c		2.5c	3.1c		4.1c	4.2c	4.3c
	1.1d				2.2d				3.1d				4.3d
					2.2e								
					2.2f								
					2.2g								

ICT

	ICT 1 finding out		ICT 2 ideas	ICT 3 reviewing	ICT 4 breadth
	1.1a	1.2a	2a	3a	4a
	1.1b	1.2b	2b	3b	4b
	1.1c	`1.2c	2c	3c	4c
		1.2d			

History

	H1 chronology	H2 events, people	H3 interpret	H4 enquire	H5 org & comm	H6 breadth
	1a	2a	3a	4a	5a	6a
	1b	2b		4b		6b
						6c
						6d

Geography

	G1.1 & G1.2 enquiry		G2 places	G3 processes	G4 environment	G5 breadth
	1.1a	1.2a	2a	3a	4a	5a
	1.1b	1.2b	2b	3b	4b	5b
	1.1c	1.2c	2c			5c
	1.1d	1.2d	2d			5d
			2e			

PE

	PE1 devel skills	PE2 apply skills	PE3 evaluate	PE4 fitness	PE5 breadth
	1a	2a	3a	4a	5a dance
	1b	2b	3b	4b	5b games
		2c	3c		5c gym

Art & Design

	A&D1 ideas	A&D2 making	A&D3 evaluating	A&D4 materials	A&D5 breadth
	1a	2a	3a	4a	5a
	1b	2b	3b	4b	5b
		2c		4c	5c
					5d

PHSE & C

	PSHEC1 conf & resp	PSHEC2 citizenship	PSHEC3 health	PSHEC4 relationships
	1a	2a	3a	4a
	1b	2b	3b	4b
	1c	2c	3c	4c
	1d	2d	3d	4d
	1e	2e	3e	4e
		2f	3f	
		2g	3g	
		2h		

D&T

	D&T 1 developing	D&T 2 tool use	D&T 3 evaluating	D&T 4 materials	D&T 5 breadth
	1a	2a	3a	4a	5a
	1b	2b	3b	4b	5b
	1c	2c			5c
	1d	2d			
	1e	2e			

Music

	M1 performing	M2 composing	M3 appraising	M4 listening	M5 breadth
	1a	2a	3a	4a	5a
	1b	2b	3b	4b	5b
	1c			4c	5c
					5d

Key to KS1 PoS on Pages 69-74

Notes on how to take the learning forward:

Critical Skills	Thinking Skills
problem solving	observing
decision making	classifying
critical thinking	prediction
creative thinking	making inferences
communication	problem solving
organisation	drawing conclusions
management	
leadership	

Drapes, Pegs and Ribbons

Drapes, Pegs and Ribbons

Previous experience in the Foundation Stage. Drapes, pegs and ribbons are all materials that are familiar in Early Years Foundation Stage settings, and most children will have used them in:

* free play indoors and outside;
* dressing up and role play areas;
* performance areas.

They will also have manipulated pegs when playing with:

* number lines;
* alphabet and other washing lines;
* washing dolls' clothes and other materials;

They may also have used pegs to hang up paintings and other work to dry.

Pause for thought

In the early stages of working with these materials it is crucial to continue to observe the children. Only by doing this can you set developmentally appropriate challenges and provocations. The ideas listed here are offered as suggestions; the most exciting challenges will arise from children's own interests and motivations, which will only become apparent as you spend time with them, watching and joining them in their play. As you do this, you will be moving between the three interconnecting roles of observer, co-player, extender described below, and will be able to decide what you need to do next to take the learning forward.

The responsive adult (see page 5)

In three interconnecting roles, the responsive adult will be:

* observing
* listening
* interpreting

observer

* **modelling**
* **playing alongside**
* **offering suggestions**
* **responding sensitively**
* **initiating with care!**

co-player

* discussing ideas
* sharing thinking
* modelling new skills
* asking open questions
* being an informed extender
* instigating ideas & thoughts
* supporting children as they make links in learning
* making possibilities evident
* introducing new ideas and resources
* offering challenges and provocations

extender

Offering challenges and provocations - some ideas:

As children get older they should be able to use ribbons, strings, fabric, drapes and other open-ended materials in role play and imaginative situations. Some children may not have had experience of using open-ended materials and may need some help at first.

? Can you use drapes, pegs and ribbons to make one of these places?
> a cafe
> a shop
> a tent or wigwam
> an ice-cream stall
> a a puppet theatre

? Use fabric, paper and recycled materials to make some costumes and props for the people who work or live in the place you have made.

? Make up some stories and characters for these settings, and make a book, a film or a powerpoint story about what happens.

? Can you use canes, boxes or recycled materials with the ribbons and drapes to make a structure with more than one room?

? Can you make some clothing, masks, wigs and hats for yourselves? Draw your designs first, then help each other to make them. Use pegs and ribbons to fasten the costumes. Can you make:
> a superhero cape
> a wig for a queen
> a costume for a pirate
> a space helmet
> a costume for a pop singer.

? Have a fashion parade, or make a photo catalogue of all your creations.

? Choose a puppet or a soft toy and use ribbons and drapes to make clothes for them.

Ready for more?

- Design some costumes for your own plays of stories such as:
  - The Elves and the Shoemaker
  - Cinderella
  - Little Red Riding Hood
  - Peter Pan and Captain Hook.

  Take photos of your inventions.

- Find some ways of joining fabrics and ribbons. Try staples, sticky tape, sewing, different types of glue. Which is best?
- Can you create a dance using the ribbons and fabrics? You could make
  - a water dance
  - a firework dance
  - a weather or seasons dance
  - a space dance.
- Print your own fabrics, flags and ribbons for role play. You could use:
  - fabric crayons or paints
  - tie dye or batik
  - printing with everyday objects
  - making your own stencils with special shapes or characters.

  You can use your fabrics to make table-cloths, cushions, curtains or hangings.

- Make your own playmats from old sheets. Use fabric crayons to make roads, farms, space or lunar scenes.
- Use fabrics to make backdrops for your play areas. You could make a Harry potter scene, Doctor Who's Tardis, a story land or a magic kingdom.

Materials, equipment suppliers, websites, books and other references

For cheap ribbon try:

* market stalls;
* florists;
* cut fabric or plastic into strips;
* look in charity and pound shops.

www.midpac.co.uk has a huge range of ribbon and other trimmings.

Get bargain rolls of masking tape, duct tape and sellotape, in pound shops.

Use old sheets or curtains for flags and banners. **Google** 'ribbon' 'flag' 'flagpole' for images.

Some **websites** for bunting and flags:

www.cottonbunting.co.uk a site with skull and crossbone bunting and lots of other designs;

www.portfolio-display.co.uk for lots of design ideas;

www.streetparty.org.uk for pictures of street parties;

www.activityvillage.co.uk for instructions and templates for making your own bunting;

www.markfennell.com/flags has pictures of flags of all countries;

http://flags.midlandimports.com sell flags of all nations;

www.mrflag.com will make a flag to your own design;

http://dharmashop.com shows lots of Tibetan prayer flags.

Some suitable **books** for younger readers include:

Purple Ribbons; Cristina Guarneri; Authorhouse

The Tent; Dorothy Jane Mills; Bookman

Camping Catastrophe; Abby Klein; Blue Sky Press

Camping; Tim Seeberg; Child's World

The Red Ribbon: A Story of Friendship by Kristine Lombardi; Readers Digest

Sleeping in a Sack: Camping Activities for Kids; Linda White; Gibbs M Smith

The Happy Campers; Kat Heyes; Bloomsbury

Go Outside!: An Activity Book for Outdoor Adventures; Nancy Blakey; Ten Speed Press

Curriculum coverage grid overleaf

Potential NC KS1 Curriculum Coverage through the provocations suggested for drapes, pegs and ribbons

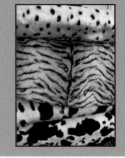

Literacy

	Lit 1 speak	Lit 2 listen	Lit 3 group	Lit 4 drama	Lit 5 word	Lit 6 spell	Lit 7 text1	Lit 8 text2	Lit 9 text3	Lit10 text4	Lit11 sentence	Lit12 presentation
	1.1	2.1	3.1	4.1	5.1	6.1	7.1	8.1	9.1	10.1	11.1	12.1
	1.2	2.2	3.2	4.2	5.2	6.2	7.2	8.2	9.2	10.2	11.2	12.2

Numeracy

	Num 1 U&A	Num 2 count	Num 3 number	Num 4 calculate	Num 5 shape	Num 6 measure	Num 7 data
	1.1	2.1	3.1	4.1	5.1	6.1	7.1
	1.2	2.2	3.2	4.2	5.2	6.2	7.2

Science

SC1 Enquiry			SC2 Life processes					SC3 Materials		SC4 Phys processes		
Sc1.1	Sc1.2	Sc1.3	Sc2.1	Sc2.2	Sc2.3	Sc2.4	Sc2.5	Sc3.1	Sc3.2	Sc4.1	Sc4.2	Sc4.3
1.1a	1.2a	1.3a	2.1a	2.2a	2.3a	2.4a	2.5a	3.1a	3.2a	4.1a	4.2a	4.3a
1.1b	1.2b	1.3b	2.1b	2.2b	2.3b	2.4b	2.5b	3.1b	3.2b	4.1b	4.2b	4.3b
1.1c	1.2c	1.3c	2.1c	2.2c	2.3c		2.5c	3.1c		4.1c	4.2c	4.3c
1.1d				2.2d				3.1d				4.3d
				2.2e								
				2.2f								
				2.2g								

ICT

	ICT 1 finding out		ICT 2 ideas	ICT 3 reviewing	ICT 4 breadth
	1.1a	1.2a	2a	3a	4a
	1.1b	1.2b	2b	3b	4b
	1.1c	1.2c	2c	3c	4c
		1.2d			

Full version of KS1 PoS on pages 69-74
Photocopiable version on page 8

D&T

	D&T 1 developing	D&T 2 tool use	D&T 3 evaluating	D&T 4 materials	D&T 5 breadth
	1a	2a	3a	4a	5a
	1b	2b	3b	4b	5b
	1c	2c			5c
	1d	2d			
	1e	2e			

History

	H1 chronology	H2 events, people	H3 interpret	H4 enquire	H5 org & comm	H6 breadth
	1a	2a	3a	4a	5a	6a
	1b	2b		4b		6b
						6c
						6d

Geography

	G1.1 & G1.2 enquiry		G2 places	G3 processes	G4 environment	G5 breadth
	1.1a	1.2a	2a	3a	4a	5a
	1.1b	1.2b	2b	3b	4b	5b
	1.1c	1.2c	2c			5c
	1.1d	1.2d	2d			5d
			2e			

Music

	M1 performing	M2 composing	M3 appraising	M4 listening	M5 breadth
	1a	2a	3a	4a	5a
	1b	2b	3b	4b	5b
	1c			4c	5c
					5d

PHSE & C

	PSHEC1 conf & resp	PSHEC2 citizenship	PSHEC3 health	PSHEC4 relationships
	1a	2a	3a	4a
	1b	2b	3b	4b
	1c	2c	3c	4c
	1d	2d	3d	4d
	1e	2e	3e	4e
		2f	3f	
		2g	3g	
		2h		

Art & Design

	A&D1 ideas	A&D2 making	A&D3 evaluating	A&D4 materials	A&D5 breadth
	1a	2a	3a	4a	5a
	1b	2b	3b	4b	5b
		2c		4c	5c
					5d

PE

	PE1 devel skills	PE2 apply skills	PE3 evaluate	PE4 fitness	PE5 breadth
	1a	2a	3a	4a	5a dance
	1b	2b	3b	4b	5b games
		2c	3c		5c gym

Critical skills	Thinking Skills
problem solving	observing
decision making	classifying
critical thinking	prediction
creative thinking	making inferences
communication	problem solving
organisation	drawing conclusions
management	
leadership	

Heroes and Villains

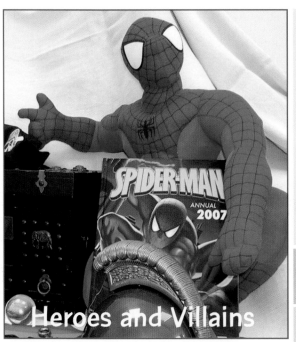

Heroes and Villains

Previous experience in the Foundation Stage

Heroes and villains are always popular with young children, specially many boys. During the Early Years Foundation Stage children will have encountered heroes and villains in:

* film, DVD, TV, computer games;
* stories, comics, picture books, cartoons;
* small world toys, play,mats, accessories;
* dressing up clothes and props;
* superhero dens and shelters;

They will have played out many of the stories and scenarios they have seen in:

* free play indoors and outside;
* dressing up activities;
* small world play;
* sand, water and construction play.

Pause for thought

In the early stages of working with these materials it is crucial to continue to observe the children. Only by doing this can you set developmentally appropriate challenges and provocations. The ideas listed here are offered as suggestions; the most exciting challenges will arise from children's own interests and motivations, which will only become apparent as you spend time with them, watching and joining them in their play. As you do this, you will be moving between the three interconnecting roles of observer, co-player, extender described below, and will be able to decide what you need to do next to take the learning forward.

The responsive adult (see page 5)

In three interconnecting roles, the responsive adult will be:

* observing
* listening
* interpreting

 observer

* **modelling**
* **playing alongside**
* **offering suggestions**
* **responding sensitively**
* **initiating with care!**

co-player

* discussing ideas
* sharing thinking
* modelling new skills
* asking open questions
* being an informed extender
* instigating ideas & thoughts
* supporting children as they make links in learning
* making possibilities evident
* introducing new ideas and resources
* offering challenges and provocations

extender

Offering challenges and provocations - some ideas:

As children enter Key Stage 1, these characters become even more important, as by this stage children find it easy to engage with fantasy and enter imagined worlds.

? Can you make up some role play stories about your favourite heroes and villains?

? Write some scripts for role plays. You could use a dictaphone or tape recorder.

? Design and make some backdrops or scenery for your role plays.

? Design and make some props and record some sound effects for the plays.

? Rehearse your role play until it is polished enough to be performed to an audience. Now invite some people to come and watch. Make some posters and tickets.

? Choose your favourite scene from a programme or book about heroes and villains and turn it into a role play.

? Find some superhero and villain figures or bring some from home. Can you make a small world for your figures, using recycled materials and other things you can find?

? Make up some games featuring superheroes and villains. You could:
  * make a card game
  * make a race game to use with dice and counters
  * make a spinner game
  * invent a team game with rules to play in the hall or playground

? Make a Heroes and Villains Treasure Hunt Game. Make some treasure to hide. Write the clues on cards and see if your friends can find the hidden treasure.

? Can you design a new vehicle for a superhero or a villain? Draw a labelled diagram of your invention, and have a competition with your friends. Ask someone to judge the best design.

Ready for more?

- Make a 'Rogues Gallery' of villains. You could use pictures from comics or the internet, or dress up and photograph the villains. Make the pictures into a book with descriptions of each character.

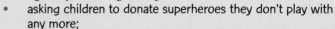

- Write a song, chant or rap about your favourite hero or villain, and include it in a play about them.

- Use a digital camcorder or camera to make films or powerpoint presentations about your role plays or small worlds.

- Print out your pictures and turn them into comic strips by adding captions and speech bubbles.

- Interview your parents or grandparents to find out who their superheroes were when they were children. perhaps they still have photos, books, comics or toys to show you.

- Use the Internet and libraries to see if you can find some pictures, video or books about these heroes and villains, such as Robin Hood, Davy Crockett, The Lone Ranger, Roy of the Rovers, Dan Dare, Supergirl etc. ** Internet access for this activity should be supervised closely.

- Talk about your personal heroes who are real people. Make a class book about real heroes, by drawing, taking photos and writing why you think they deserve to be included.

Materials, equipment suppliers, websites, books and other references

You can get superhero figures by:
- asking children to donate superheroes they don't play with any more;
- asking older children in the school to donate figures;
- looking in Charity shops or on Ebay;
- buying some knights in armour, pirates or space heroes.

Or make your own costumes with fabrics, pegs and elastic. Buy some non-fraying fabric in superhero colours and cut into capes, headbands and flags. **Pound or bargain shops** often have dressing up props for superheroes.

Google Images 'pirate' 'superhero' 'knights in armour' 'cardboard box castle' 'Star Wars figure'.

www.make-stuff.com/kids - has some great projects including a cardboard castle;

www.terragenesis.co.uk - model castle using textured paint;

www.ecocentric.co.uk - sell a model castle and other toys made from recycled cardboard.

Some suitable **books** for younger readers include:

Fiction	**Harry Potter**: Heroes and Villains; Penguin Character Books
	Spilling the Beans: Historical Heroes and Vintage Villains; Miles Kelly Publishing Ltd
	Spider-Man 3: Meet the Heroes and Villains; Harry Lime, Steven E. Gordon; HarperTrophy
	King Kong: Journey to Skull Island; Jennifer Frantz; Harper Collins
	My Parents Think I'm Sleeping; Jack Prelutsky; HarperTrophy
	Stories of Pirates; Russell Punter; Usborne
	The Secret Superhero; Tony Ross; Hodder Children's
	How to Be a Superhero; Michael D'Agostino; Trafford
	Hercules: Superhero; Collins Big Cat; Diana Redmond; Chris Mould; Collins
Non Fiction	**Heroes and Villains of History 55 BC-1216 AD**; Les Ives; Colour History
	The Children's Book of Heroes; **William J. Bennett**; Simon and Schuster
	Heroes and Villains; Pat Moon, Kaye Umansky; Hodder
	The Usborne Book of Dressing Up; Chris Caudron; Usborne
	The Dressing Up Book; Jane Bull Dorling Kindersley
	The Barefoot Book of Pirates (Book & CD); Barefoot Books
	Pirates and Other Adventures (Role-play in the Early Years); Jo Boulton;David Fulton

Curriculum coverage grid overleaf

Potential NC KS1 Curriculum Coverage through the provocations suggested for heroes and villains

Full version of KS1 PoS on pages 69-74
Photocopiable version on page 8

Literacy

	Lit 1 speak	Lit 2 listen	Lit 3 group	Lit 4 drama	Lit 5 word	Lit 6 spell	Lit 7 text1	Lit 8 text2	Lit 9 text3	Lit10 text4	Lit11 sentence	Lit12 presentation
	1.1	2.1	3.1	4.1	5.1	6.1	7.1	8.1	9.1	10.1	11.1	12.1
	1.2	2.2	3.2	4.2	5.2	6.2	7.2	8.2	9.2	10.2	11.2	12.2

Numeracy

	Num 1 U&A	Num 2 count	Num 3 number	Num 4 calculate	Num 5 shape	Num 6 measure	Num 7 data
	1.1	2.1	3.1	4.1	5.1	6.1	7.1
	1.2	2.2	3.2	4.2	5.2	6.2	7.2

Science

	SC1 Enquiry			SC2 Life processes					SC3 Materials		SC4 Phys processes		
	Sc1.1	Sc1.2	Sc1.3	Sc2.1	Sc2.2	Sc2.3	Sc2.4	Sc2.5	Sc3.1	Sc3.2	Sc4.1	Sc4.2	Sc4.3
	1.1a	1.2a	1.3a	2.1a	2.2a	2.3a	2.4a	2.5a	3.1a	3.2a	4.1a	4.2a	4.3a
	1.1b	1.2b	1.3b	2.1b	2.2b	2.3b	2.4b	2.5b	3.1b	3.2b	4.1b	4.2b	4.3b
	1.1c	1.2c	1.3c	2.1c	2.2c	2.3c		2.5c	3.1c		4.1c	4.2c	4.3c
	1.1d				2.2d				3.1d				4.3d
					2.2e								
					2.2f								
					2.2g								

ICT

	ICT 1 finding out		ICT 2 ideas	ICT 3 reviewing	ICT 4 breadth
	1.1a	1.2a	2a	3a	4a
	1.1b	1.2b	2b	3b	4b
	1.1c	1.2c	2c	3c	4c
		1.2d			

D&T

	D&T 1 developing	D&T 2 tool use	D&T 3 evaluating	D&T 4 materials	D&T 5 breadth
	1a	2a	3a	4a	5a
	1b	2b	3b	4b	5b
	1c	2c			5c
	1d	2d			
	1e	2e			

History

	H1 chronology	H2 events, people	H3 interpret	H4 enquire	H5 org & comm	H6 breadth
	1a	2a	3a	4a	5a	6a
	1b	2b		4b		6b
						6c
						6d

Geography

	G1.1 & G1.2 enquiry		G2 places	G3 processes	G4 environment	G5 breadth
	1.1a	1.2a	2a	3a	4a	5a
	1.1b	1.2b	2b	3b	4b	5b
	1.1c	1.2c	2c			5c
	1.1d	1.2d	2d			5d
			2e			

Music

	M1 performing	M2 composing	M3 appraising	M4 listening	M5 breadth
	1a	2a	3a	4a	5a
	1b	2b	3b	4b	5b
	1c			4c	5c
					5d

PHSE & C

	PSHEC1 conf & resp	PSHEC2 citizenship	PSHEC3 health	PSHEC4 relationships
	1a	2a	3a	4a
	1b	2b	3b	4b
	1c	2c	3c	4c
	1d	2d	3d	4d
	1e	2e	3e	4e
		2f	3f	
		2g	3g	
		2h		

Art & Design

	A&D1 ideas	A&D2 making	A&D3 evaluating	A&D4 materials	A&D5 breadth
	1a	2a	3a	4a	5a
	1b	2b	3b	4b	5b
		2c		4c	5c
					5d

PE

	PE1 devel skills	PE2 apply skills	PE3 evaluate	PE4 fitness	PE5 breadth
	1a	2a	3a	4a	5a dance
	1b	2b	3b	4b	5b games
		2c	3c		5c gym

Critical skills	Thinking Skills
problem solving	observing
decision making	classifying
critical thinking	prediction
creative thinking	making inferences
communication	problem solving
organisation	drawing conclusions
management	
leadership	

Shops and Cafes

Shops and Cafes

Previous experience in the Foundation Stage

Making and playing with shops and meals is a favourite of children from their earliest years. They will have had experience of:

* role play in home corners and areas;
* informal play in their own shops;
* structured shopping play with money and goods, often accompanied by adults;
* real experience of shopping on walks and visits with practitioners and parents;
* making cafes and other eating places for play in role;
* making pretend food from dough, clay and other materials for shopping and domestic play.
* cooking food for snack times and special occasions.

Pause for thought

In the early stages of working with these materials it is crucial to continue to observe the children. Only by doing this can you set developmentally appropriate challenges and provocations. The ideas listed here are offered as suggestions; the most exciting challenges will arise from children's own interests and motivations, which will only become apparent as you spend time with them, watching and joining them in their play. As you do this, you will be moving between the three interconnecting roles of observer, co-player, extender described below, and will be able to decide what you need to do next to take the learning forward.

The responsive adult (see page 5)

In three interconnecting roles, the responsive adult will be:

* observing
* listening
* interpreting

observer

* **modelling**
* **playing alongside**
* **offering suggestions**
* **responding sensitively**
* **initiating with care!**

co-player

* discussing ideas
* sharing thinking
* modelling new skills
* asking open questions
* being an informed extender
* instigating ideas & thoughts
* supporting children as they make links in learning
* making possibilities evident
* introducing new ideas and resources
* offering challenges and provocations

extender

Offering challenges and provocations - some ideas:

Children will need to continue their informal and freely imagined role play with shops and making 'food' with a range of malleable materials. This experience should continue alongside the more challenging work on provocations and adult initiated tasks.

? Find some clay or dough and see if you can make replica food. Can you make your materials into:
  * fast food such as pizzas, fish and chips, kebabs, burgers
  * different sorts of bread such as pitta bread, rolls, French sticks, big brown loaves
  * cakes and buns
  * vegetables such as carrots, cabbages, potatoes.

? Now can you use boxes or a table to make a shop or cafe where you can sell your food. You will need to make price labels, and find some real or plastic money. You will also need some customers.

? Work with some friends to make a snack shop. You could make some simple biscuits or buns, or put icing or cream cheese on bought biscuits. You could make a fruit shop if your school has a Fruit Scheme or Healthy Eating focus.

? Look on Google Images for some shop signs and logos. Print them or copy them, and use them to make a shop in your classroom.

? Find a simple recipe book and make some dips to eat with crisps or tortilla chips. Make a cafe where your friends can come for a snack.

? Use paper plates and recycled materials to make some fake plates of food. You could use painted dry pasta, beads or seeds to make meals. You could make pasta with string, or bread from thin foam. See how many different meals you can make.

Ready for more?

🔥 Make some salt dough from flour, salt and water. Make the dough into food such as cakes, pies, fruit or vegetables. Bake the dough food till it is hard, then paint it and varnish it with PVA mixed with water. Use the food for pretend meals or shops.

🔥 Find some stories about food and shopping. Read some of these and then make a shop or house where you can turn the story into a play.

🔥 Make some buns, biscuits or cakes and sell them to your friends in a shop or snack cafe.

🔥 Make a miniature picnic for small world people using card, paper, paint, felt pens, dough or found and recycled materials.

🔥 Use a sheet or shower curtain to make a background for a shop or home area. Paint a big picture on it with:
  - furniture, windows, TV and other objects for a house;
  - shelves and piles of cans or bottles for a supermarket or shop;
  - umbrellas and outdoor furniture for a barbecue or picnic.

🔥 Make a Charity Shop in your classroom. Choose a charity to give the money to, then ask friends and your families to donate things to sell in your shop. Invite other children and adults to come and buy the things, and send the money to your chosen charity.

Materials, equipment suppliers, websites, books and other references

Educational suppliers all have a range of plastic replicas of fruit and vegetables. - try www.tts-group.co.uk www.ascoeducational.co.uk or **your local consortium group**.
Make your own fake food (fruit, vegetables, plates of food, pizzas etc) using a simple flour and salt dough recipe. Look for ideas on the internet - at www.gigglemoose.com/salt_dough_recipe or www.easy-child-crafts.com/salt-dough-recipes or just put 'salt dough recipe' in Google or another search engine.

Look on **Google Images** 'salt dough' 'dough sculpture' 'shops' 'kids shops'.
For information on Healthy Eating and the Free Fruit Scheme try:
www.dh.gov.uk/en/Publicationsandstatistics/Publications/PublicationsPolicyAndGuidance/DH Fruit Scheme where you will find a leaflet to download. Or try:
www.dh.gov.uk/en/Publichealth/Healthimprovement/FiveADay/FiveADaygeneralinformation or www.5aday.nhs.uk nhs site for fruit scheme for more information

Some suitable **books** for younger readers include:
I Will Never Not Ever Eat a Tomato; Lauren Child; Candlewick Press
Oliver's Vegetables, Oliver's Fruit Salad; Vivian French; Hodder Children's Books
Handa's Surprise; Eileen Browne; Walker Books
The Giant Jam Sandwich; John Vernon; Piper Picture Books
Mrs Wobble the Waitress; Allan Ahlberg; Puffin Books
Master Bun the Baker's Boy; Allan Ahlberg; Walker Books
Shirley's Shops; Allan Ahlberg; Walker Books
Trouble at the Dinosaur Café; Brian Moses; Puffin Books
Joe's Café; Rose Impey; Orchard Books
Kangaroo's CanCan Café; Julia Jarman; Orchard Books
Down at the Seaweed Café; Robert Perry; Raincoast Books
Kids' First Cook Book; Dorling Kindersley
My Cake; Sheila Gore; A & C Black
Easy Peasy: Real Food For Kids Who Want to Cook; Mary Contini; Ebury Press
Children's Quick and Easy Cookbook; Angela Wilkes; Dorling Kindersley
The Little Book of Dough; Lynn Garner; Featherstone Education
Salt Dough; Laura Torres; American Girl
Fun Dough: Over 100 Salt Dough Projects for All the Family; Brenda Porteous
Salt Dough Fun; Brigitte Casagranda; Gareth Stevens Publishing

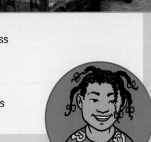

Curriculum coverage grid overleaf

Potential NC KS1 Curriculum Coverage through the provocations suggested for shops and cafes

Full version of KS1 PoS on pages 69-74
Photocopiable version on page 8

Literacy

	Lit 1 speak	Lit 2 listen	Lit 3 group	Lit 4 drama	Lit 5 word	Lit 6 spell	Lit 7 text1	Lit 8 text2	Lit 9 text3	Lit10 text4	Lit11 sentence	Lit12 presentation
Literacy	1.1	2.1	3.1	4.1	5.1	6.1	7.1	8.1	9.1	10.1	11.1	12.1
	1.2	2.2	3.2	4.2	5.2	6.2	7.2	8.2	9.2	10.2	11.2	12.2

Numeracy

	Num 1 U&A	Num 2 count	Num 3 number	Num 4 calculate	Num 5 shape	Num 6 measure	Num 7 data
Numeracy	1.1	2.1	3.1	4.1	5.1	6.1	7.1
	1.2	2.2	3.2	4.2	5.2	6.2	7.2

Science

	SC1 Enquiry			SC2 Life processes					SC3 Materials		SC4 Phys processes		
	Sc1.1	Sc1.2	Sc1.3	Sc2.1	Sc2.2	Sc2.3	Sc2.4	Sc2.5	Sc3.1	Sc3.2	Sc4.1	Sc4.2	Sc4.3
Science	1.1a	1.2a	1.3a	2.1a	2.2a	2.3a	2.4a	2.5a	3.1a	3.2a	4.1a	4.2a	4.3a
	1.1b	1.2b	1.3b	2.1b	2.2b	2.3b	2.4b	2.5b	3.1b	3.2b	4.1b	4.2b	4.3b
	1.1c	1.2c	1.3c	2.1c	2.2c	2.3c		2.5c	3.1c		4.1c	4.2c	4.3c
	1.1d				2.2d				3.1d				4.3d
					2.2e								
					2.2f								
					2.2g								

ICT

	ICT 1 finding out		ICT 2 ideas	ICT 3 reviewing	ICT 4 breadth
ICT	1.1a	1.2a	2a	3a	4a
	1.1b	1.2b	2b	3b	4b
	1.1c	1.2c	2c	3c	4c
		1.2d			

D&T

	D&T 1 developing	D&T 2 tool use	D&T 3 evaluating	D&T 4 materials	D&T 5 breadth
D&T	1a	2a	3a	4a	5a
	1b	2b	3b	4b	5b
	1c	2c			5c
	1d	2d			
	1e	2e			

History

	H1 chronology	H2 events, people	H3 interpret	H4 enquire	H5 org & comm	H6 breadth
History	1a	2a	3a	4a	5a	6a
	1b	2b		4b		6b
						6c
						6d

Geography

	G1.1 & G1.2 enquiry		G2 places	G3 processes	G4 environment	G5 breadth
Geography	1.1a	1.2a	2a	3a	4a	5a
	1.1b	1.2b	2b	3b	4b	5b
	1.1c	1.2c	2c			5c
	1.1d	1.2d	2d			5d
			2e			

Music

	M1 performing	M2 composing	M3 appraising	M4 listening	M5 breadth
Music	1a	2a	3a	4a	5a
	1b	2b	3b	4b	5b
	1c			4c	5c
					5d

PHSE & C

	PSHEC1 conf & resp	PSHEC2 citizenship	PSHEC3 health	PSHEC4 relationships
PHSE & C	1a	2a	3a	4a
	1b	2b	3b	4b
	1c	2c	3c	4c
	1d	2d	3d	4d
	1e	2e	3e	4e
		2f	3f	
		2g	3g	
		2h		

Art & Design

	A&D1 ideas	A&D2 making	A&D3 evaluating	A&D4 materials	A&D5 breadth
Art & Design	1a	2a	3a	4a	5a
	1b	2b	3b	4b	5b
		2c		4c	5c
					5d

PE

	PE1 devel skills	PE2 apply skills	PE3 evaluate	PE4 fitness	PE5 breadth
PE	1a	2a	3a	4a	5a dance
	1b	2b	3b	4b	5b games
		2c	3c		5c gym

Critical skills	Thinking Skills
problem solving	observing
decision making	classifying
critical thinking	prediction
creative thinking	making inferences
communication	problem solving
organisation	drawing conclusions
management	
leadership	

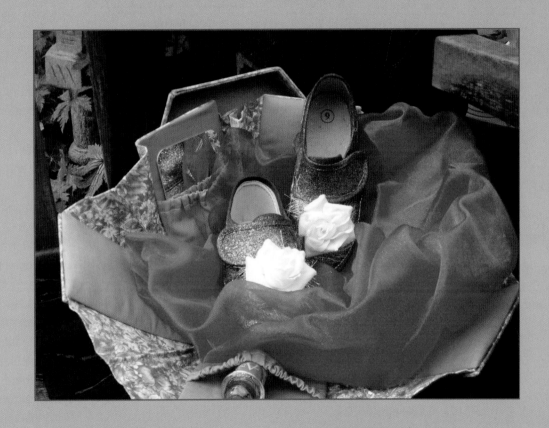

Bags and Boxes

Bags and Boxes

Previous experience in the Foundation Stage

During their time in the Early Years Foundation Stage, children will have explored bags, boxes and other containers:
* in free play indoors and out of doors.

and to:
* explore outdoor play activities including carrying things on wheeled toys;
* re-enact stories;
* support role play activities;
* transport objects and toys;
* make collections of objects, indoors and outside;
* bring activities indoors or take them outside.

They should also have experienced the use of Story Bags and boxes independently and in more formal sessions.

Pause for thought

In the early stages of working with these materials it is crucial to continue to observe the children. Only by doing this can you set developmentally appropriate challenges and provocations. The ideas listed here are offered as suggestions; the most exciting challenges will arise from children's own interests and motivations, which will only become apparent as you spend time with them, watching and joining them in their play. As you do this, you will be moving between the three interconnecting roles of observer, coplayer, extender described below, and will be able to decide what you need to do next to take the learning forward.

The responsive adult (see page 5)

In three interconnecting roles, the responsive adult will be:

* observing
* listening
* interpreting

 observer

* **modelling**
* **playing alongside**
* **offering suggestions**
* **responding sensitively**
* **initiating with care!**

co-player

* discussing ideas
* sharing thinking
* modelling new skills
* asking open questions
* being an informed extender
* instigating ideas & thoughts
* supporting children as they make links in learning
* making possibilities evident
* introducing new ideas and resources
* offering challenges and provocations

extender

Offering challenges and provocations - some ideas:

It is useful to have a wide range of different containers available for children to use independently, or for filling with challenging and inspiring resources to inspire play.

? Find a bag or box and fill it with six objects. Use these objects to make up a story. Take photos or draw the objects to illustrate your story.

? How many different kinds of containers can you find:
  * boxes
  * baskets
  * bowls and buckets
  * bags

Choose one and turn it into a treasure box by collecting special things.

? Work together to make some bags or boxes for different sorts of people. Fill them with clothing and pops for each character:
  * workers, such as window cleaners, builders, decorators, hairdressers etc.
  * unusual jobs, such as explorers, spacemen, circus performers, puppeteers, birdwatchers, bug collectors
  * entertainers, such as pop singers, actors, mime artists, actors or singers
  * historical characters such as Victorians, Romans, kings and queens.

Use your bags to make plays and other performances for your friends and other classes.

? Make some small world boxes with animals, play people, fabrics, and other objects to make scenes for the small worlds. You could try:
  * a jungle box
  * a fairy story box
  * a space box.

Ready for more?

- Can you make a prop box for one of these people:
  - a doctor or nurse
  - a mechanic
  - a dancer
  - a vet
  - a headteacher
  - an inventor.
- Can you make a box for a conjuror? Look in books or on the internet for the things a magician needs. Make a cloak and find a hat for them to wear. Now learn some magic tricks to show your friends.
- Collect some shoes, find some carrier bags and ask a shoe shop for some shoe boxes. Use these to make a shoe shop. Make price lists and notices, and play a shopping game. Find out where to get a foot measure so the shoes are the right size.
- Can you make a perfumed bag or a bag that makes sounds?
- Use the Internet to find out about the special sorts of bags that are used by some workers. Find out what is inside a bag for:
  - an airline pilot
  - a person who defuses bombs
  - a rescue team
  - an ambulance worker
- Choose a favourite story and collect the objects you need to make a story box to go with the story. Now act the story out, using the props in your story bag.

Materials, equipment suppliers, websites, books and other references

Charity shops and rummage sales are great sources of clothes for dressing up. Add some hats, shoes, jewellery and other accessories and the children will do the rest! You can also offer lengths of fabric and clothes pegs to fasten them with. Get remnants and odd lengths of fabric, lace, braid, ribbons, trimming and other desirable items from:

- parents and friends
- market stalls and cheap fabric shops

Collect a selection of bags and boxes by looking out for:

- unwanted sports bags and lunch boxes
- gift bags and boxes
- baskets and other containers with lids
- interesting boxes from junk shops and charity shops
- asking parents, colleagues, family and friends to save interesting containers

Some **web sites**:

www.thriftyfun.com - for ideas of making containers from all sorts of things;

www.holyspiritinteractive.net/kids/artsncrafts - click through to making boxes for instructions on making different shapes and kinds of boxes, with templates;

www.artistshelpingchildren.org - instructions for making and using all sorts of boxes;

www.savvysource.com - is an encyclopedia of craft ideas;

www.earlyyearsresources.co.uk have play food, shopping baskets and furniture.

Google Images - 'boxes' 'decorated boxes' 'decorative boxes' 'gift boxes' for hundreds of ideas

Some **book** titles:

The Little Book of Prop Boxes for Role Play; Ann Roberts; Featherstone Education

Making Make-believe: Props, Costumes and Play Ideas; MaryAnn F. Kohl; Gryphon House

Earth-friendly Wearables: How to Make Fabulous Clothes and Accessories from Reusable Objects; George Pfiffner; Jossey Bass

Fabric Leftovers: Simple, Adaptable Ways to Use Scraps; D'Arcy-Jean Milne; C & T Publishing

Galileo's Treasure Box; Catherine Brighton; Walker

Role-play Activities (Early Years Activity Chest); Chris Heald; Scholastic

Making Cool Crafts and Awesome Art: A Kid's Treasure Trove of Fabulous Fun Roberta Gould; Williamson

Curriculum coverage grid overleaf

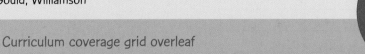

Potential NC KS1 Curriculum Coverage through the provocations suggested for bags and boxes

Literacy	Lit 1 speak	Lit 2 listen	Lit 3 group	Lit 4 drama	Lit 5 word	Lit 6 spell	Lit 7 text1	Lit 8 text2	Lit 9 text3	Lit10 text4	Lit11 sentence	Lit12 presentation
	1.1	2.1	3.1	4.1	5.1	6.1	7.1	8.1	9.1	10.1	11.1	12.1
	1.2	2.2	3.2	4.2	5.2	6.2	7.2	8.2	9.2	10.2	11.2	12.2

Numeracy	Num 1 U&A	Num 2 count	Num 3 number	Num 4 calculate	Num 5 shape	Num 6 measure	Num 7 data
	1.1	2.1	3.1	4.1	5.1	6.1	7.1
	1.2	2.2	3.2	4.2	5.2	6.2	7.2

Full version of KS1 PoS on pages 69-74
Photocopiable version on page 8

Science	SC1 Enquiry			SC2 Life processes					SC3 Materials		SC4 Phys processes		
	Sc1.1	Sc1.2	Sc1.3	Sc2.1	Sc2.2	Sc2.3	Sc2.4	Sc2.5	Sc3.1	Sc3.2	Sc4.1	Sc4.2	Sc4.3
	1.1a	1.2a	1.3a	2.1a	2.2a	2.3a	2.4a	2.5a	3.1a	3.2a	4.1a	4.2a	4.3a
	1.1b	1.2b	1.3b	2.1b	2.2b	2.3b	2.4b	2.5b	3.1b	3.2b	4.1b	4.2b	4.3b
	1.1c	1.2c	1.3c	2.1c	2.2c	2.3c		2.5c	3.1c		4.1c	4.2c	4.3c
	1.1d				2.2d				3.1d				4.3d
					2.2e								
					2.2f								
					2.2g								

ICT	ICT 1 finding out		ICT 2 ideas	ICT 3 reviewing	ICT 4 breadth
	1.1a	1.2a	2a	3a	4a
	1.1b	1.2b	2b	3b	4b
	1.1c	1.2c	2c	3c	4c
		1.2d			

D&T	D&T 1 developing	D&T 2 tool use	D&T 3 evaluating	D&T 4 materials	D&T 5 breadth
	1a	2a	3a	4a	5a
	1b	2b	3b	4b	5b
	1c	2c			5c
	1d	2d			
	1e	2e			

History	H1 chronology	H2 events, people	H3 interpret	H4 enquire	H5 org & comm	H6 breadth
	1a	2a	3a	4a	5a	6a
	1b	2b		4b		6b
						6c
						6d

Geography	G1.1 & G1.2 enquiry		G2 places	G3 processes	G4 environment	G5 breadth
	1.1a	1.2a	2a	3a	4a	5a
	1.1b	1.2b	2b	3b	4b	5b
	1.1c	1.2c	2c			5c
	1.1d	1.2d	2d			5d
			2e			

Music	M1 performing	M2 composing	M3 appraising	M4 listening	M5 breadth
	1a	2a	3a	4a	5a
	1b	2b	3b	4b	5b
	1c			4c	5c
					5d

PHSE & C	PSHEC1 conf & resp	PSHEC2 citizenship	PSHEC3 health	PSHEC4 relationships
	1a	2a	3a	4a
	1b	2b	3b	4b
	1c	2c	3c	4c
	1d	2d	3d	4d
	1e	2e	3e	4e
		2f	3f	
		2g	3g	
		2h		

Art & Design	A&D1 ideas	A&D2 making	A&D3 evaluating	A&D4 materials	A&D5 breadth
	1a	2a	3a	4a	5a
	1b	2b	3b	4b	5b
		2c		4c	5c
					5d

PE	PE1 devel skills	PE2 apply skills	PE3 evaluate	PE4 fitness	PE5 breadth
	1a	2a	3a	4a	5a dance
	1b	2b	3b	4b	5b games
		2c	3c		5c gym

Critical skills	Thinking Skills
problem solving	observing
decision making	classifying
critical thinking	prediction
creative thinking	making inferences
communication	problem solving
organisation	drawing conclusions
management	
leadership	

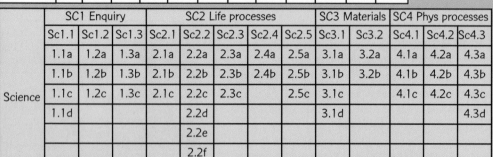

Books and Stories

Books and Stories

Previous experience in the Foundation Stage. Role playing stories is a key feature of Early Years Foundation Stage practice, and most children, will have experienced story role play in:

* adult focused activities;
* free play indoors and outside.

These role plays may have been inspired by:

* traditional stories and folk tales;
* nursery rhymes and counting rhymes;
* picture books;
* stories from TV and film;
* real life stories told by the children.

They might have worked with:

* prop boxes;
* story bags, sacks and boxes;
* small world figures;
* puppets and soft toys.

Pause for thought

In the early stages of working with these materials it is crucial to continue to observe the children. Only by doing this can you set developmentally appropriate challenges and provocations. The ideas listed here are offered as suggestions; the most exciting challenges will arise from children's own interests and motivations, which will only become apparent as you spend time with them, watching and joining them in their play. As you do this, you will be moving between the three interconnecting roles of observer, co-player, extender described below, and will be able to decide what you need to do next to take the learning forward.

The responsive adult (see page 5)

In three interconnecting roles, the responsive adult will be:

* observing
* listening
* interpreting

observer

* modelling
* playing alongside
* offering suggestions
* responding sensitively
* initiating with care!

co-player

* discussing ideas
* sharing thinking
* modelling new skills
* asking open questions
* being an informed extender
* instigating ideas & thoughts
* supporting children as they make links in learning
* making possibilities evident
* introducing new ideas and resources
* offering challenges and provocations

extender

Offering challenges and provocations - some ideas:

Children love collecting and making props for story telling. Make sure there are plenty of materials and space for this sort of construction and invention. Some children will become absorbed in making replicas as close to the original story or pictures as possible, others will be content with approximations!

? Choose a favourite story and design a box or bag to contain props and costumes for playing it. These could be:
  * small world figures
  * puppets
  * pictures
  * objects.

? Use paper or fabric to make a costume or a mask for your favourite story character.

? Can you make a 'storyteller's chair' by using a classroom chair and decorating it with all sorts of things to make it a special chair. Take turns being the story teller as the others play out the story.

? Can you make a poster for a story telling or role play performance of a favourite story? Try these:
  * Handa's Surprise
  * Elmer
  * The Gruffalo
  * Harry Potter
  * James and the Giant Peach.

? Make up some sequels to familiar traditional stories:
  What happened to Red Riding Hood on her way home?
  How did Jack spend all the money he got from the giant?
  What happened next to Max in Where the Wild Things Are?
  What happened when Spiderman met Cinderella?
  How could your favourite story end in a different way?
  What powers would you choose if you became a superhero?
  Where would you go in the Tardis?

Ready for more?

- Can you make up a play for:
  - two people?
  - three people?
  - four people?
  - more than ten people?
- Do a survey of all your class to find out which is the most popular story. When you have collected the information, make up a play based on the favourite.
- Make a book of character portraits by copying the character pictures from the books and writing or word processing a description of each one.
- See how many stories you can find in your school, at home and the library about:
  - islands
  - rescues
  - space
  - giants
  - animals.
- ADULT INPUT
  - Leave messages for the children from characters in their favourite stories;
  - Collect some props for a favourite story, to encourage role playing;
  - Have a Mystery Bag with a prop or hint about a favourite story, so the children can guess which story is in the bag.
  - Make up stories about the things that happen to you and to the children. Play them out together.

Materials, equipment suppliers, websites, books and other references

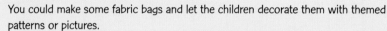

Try to find some unusual or interesting containers for books, especially if children will be using them out of doors. You could collect:
- boxes and bags
- baskets of all sorts
- drawstring fabric bags
- satchels, backpacks and sportsbags
- boxes with locks and keys

Then you or the children could then add soft toys, puppets and other objects to help the role play.

You could make some fabric bags and let the children decorate them with themed patterns or pictures.

www.threebearsplaythings.co.uk sell a pack of ten fabric collection bags for £6:50. They also have role play fabrics, barrier tape (the stripey sort), ribbon and lots more role play stuff at good prices.

www.tts-group.co.uk also have a great role play cloaks set, pirate chest, role play trolley, tabards, masks, screens, backgrounds for play,

Any story that interests the children can be the basis for a 'play' or role play activity, either 'whole body' or with puppets, soft toys or small world.

A few books for adults about role play with children are:

Role Play; Judith Harries; Step Forward
Drama and Role-play; Nichola Rees; Scholastic
Beginning Drama 4-11 ; Joe Winston; David Fulton
The Dressing Up Book ; Jane Bull DK
Usborne Book of Fancy Dress; Ray Gibson; Usborne
Empowering Your Pupils Through Role-play: Rosanna Morales; Routledge
Songs for Role Play; Jean Evans; Sally Scott ; Scholastic
Pirates and Other Adventures, Teddy Bears' Picnic, Toymaker's Workshop (Role-play in the Early Years); Jo Boulton; David Fulton - simple books with drama sessions complete with ideas, props and stories

Curriculum coverage grid overleaf

Potential NC KS1 Curriculum Coverage through the provocations suggested for books and stories

Full version of KS1 PoS on pages 69-74
Photocopiable version on page 8

Literacy

	Lit 1 speak	Lit 2 listen	Lit 3 group	Lit 4 drama	Lit 5 word	Lit 6 spell	Lit 7 text1	Lit 8 text2	Lit 9 text3	Lit10 text4	Lit11 sentence	Lit12 presentation
Literacy	1.1	2.1	3.1	4.1	5.1	6.1	7.1	8.1	9.1	10.1	11.1	12.1
	1.2	2.2	3.2	4.2	5.2	6.2	7.2	8.2	9.2	10.2	11.2	12.2

Numeracy

	Num 1 U&A	Num 2 count	Num 3 number	Num 4 calculate	Num 5 shape	Num 6 measure	Num 7 data
Numeracy	1.1	2.1	3.1	4.1	5.1	6.1	7.1
	1.2	2.2	3.2	4.2	5.2	6.2	7.2

Science

	SC1 Enquiry			SC2 Life processes					SC3 Materials		SC4 Phys processes		
	Sc1.1	Sc1.2	Sc1.3	Sc2.1	Sc2.2	Sc2.3	Sc2.4	Sc2.5	Sc3.1	Sc3.2	Sc4.1	Sc4.2	Sc4.3
Science	1.1a	1.2a	1.3a	2.1a	2.2a	2.3a	2.4a	2.5a	3.1a	3.2a	4.1a	4.2a	4.3a
	1.1b	1.2b	1.3b	2.1b	2.2b	2.3b	2.4b	2.5b	3.1b	3.2b	4.1b	4.2b	4.3b
	1.1c	1.2c	1.3c	2.1c	2.2c	2.3c		2.5c	3.1c		4.1c	4.2c	4.3c
	1.1d				2.2d				3.1d				4.3d
					2.2e								
					2.2f								
					2.2g								

ICT

	ICT 1 finding out		ICT 2 ideas	ICT 3 reviewing	ICT 4 breadth
	1.1a	1.2a	2a	3a	4a
ICT	1.1b	1.2b	2b	3b	4b
	1.1c	1.2c	2c	3c	4c
		1.2d			

D&T

	D&T 1 developing	D&T 2 tool use	D&T 3 evaluating	D&T 4 materials	D&T 5 breadth
	1a	2a	3a	4a	5a
D&T	1b	2b	3b	4b	5b
	1c	2c			5c
	1d	2d			
	1e	2e			

History

	H1 chronology	H2 events, people	H3 interpret	H4 enquire	H5 org & comm	H6 breadth
	1a	2a	3a	4a	5a	6a
History	1b	2b		4b		6b
						6c
						6d

Geography

	G1.1 & G1.2 enquiry		G2 places	G3 processes	G4 environment	G5 breadth
	1.1a	1.2a	2a	3a	4a	5a
Geography	1.1b	1.2b	2b	3b	4b	5b
	1.1c	1.2c	2c			5c
	1.1d	1.2d	2d			5d
			2e			

Music

	M1 performing	M2 composing	M3 appraising	M4 listening	M5 breadth
	1a	2a	3a	4a	5a
Music	1b	2b	3b	4b	5b
	1c			4c	5c
					5d

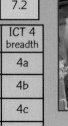

O JE DIVA

PHSE & C

	PSHEC1 conf & resp	PSHEC2 citizenship	PSHEC3 health	PSHEC4 relationships
	1a	2a	3a	4a
	1b	2b	3b	4b
PHSE & C	1c	2c	3c	4c
	1d	2d	3d	4d
	1e	2e	3e	4e
		2f	3f	
		2g	3g	
		2h		

Art & Design

	A&D1 ideas	A&D2 making	A&D3 evaluating	A&D4 materials	A&D5 breadth
	1a	2a	3a	4a	5a
Art & Design	1b	2b	3b	4b	5b
		2c		4c	5c
					5d

PE

	PE1 devel skills	PE2 apply skills	PE3 evaluate	PE4 fitness	PE5 breadth
	1a	2a	3a	4a	5a dance
PE	1b	2b	3b	4b	5b games
		2c	3c		5c gym

Critical skills	Thinking Skills
problem solving	observing
decision making	classifying
critical thinking	prediction
creative thinking	making inferences
communication	problem solving
organisation	drawing conclusions
management	
leadership	

Imagined Worlds

Imagined Worlds

Previous experience in the Foundation Stage

Inventing and experiencing imagined worlds will have been a favourite activity for many children. They will have invented their own worlds for:

* role play indoors and outside;
* small world figures and vehicles;
* stories and pictures.

and may also have:

* responded to imagined words in stories;
* invented dances and movement in response to music and other stimuli;
* taken part in plays and other dramatic activities where imagined worlds are involved;
* watched imagined worlds on TV and in films.

Pause for thought

In the early stages of working with these materials it is crucial to continue to observe the children. Only by doing this can you set developmentally appropriate challenges and provocations. The ideas listed here are offered as suggestions; the most exciting challenges will arise from children's own interests and motivations, which will only become apparent as you spend time with them, watching and joining them in their play. As you do this, you will be moving between the three interconnecting roles of observer, co-player, extender described below, and will be able to decide what you need to do next to take the learning forward.

The responsive adult (see page 5)

In three interconnecting roles, the responsive adult will be:

observer

* observing
* listening
* interpreting

co-player

* **modelling**
* **playing alongside**
* **offering suggestions**
* **responding sensitively**
* **initiating with care!**

extender

* discussing ideas
* sharing thinking
* modelling new skills
* asking open questions
* being an informed extender
* instigating ideas & thoughts
* supporting children as they make links in learning
* making possibilities evident
* introducing new ideas and resources
* offering challenges and provocations

Offering challenges and provocations - some ideas:

Provide children with a wide range of multi-purpose resources, including fabrics, boxes, canes and sticks with suitable fixing materials and objects for decoration.

? Find a box and use it to make a miniature imagined world for a superhero or film character toy.

? Use some fabrics and canes or sticks to make a structure big enough to get inside. Now make the inside of your shelter into an imagined world - what could you use?

? Get a big sheet of paper or plain fabric (an old sheet would be good). Put the fabric on the floor indoors or outside and use paint to make a big picture of an imagined world. You can put anything in your picture! When it is finished, use the picture as a backdrop for a play or reading a story.

? Make up a story about a new world. Now draw the new world and make a 3D model of it with recycled materials. Now make a film of your story, using models and small characters.

? Draw a character from your imagined world. Label the drawing to explain their clothing, jewellery, tools and equipment. Now use recycled materials to make a costume for yourself so you can be the person from another world.

? Use card or other materials to make some puppets or fantasy moving figures. Use these to make a play, a puppet show or a shadow theatre. Look up 'shadow puppets' in Google images for some really good ideas.

? Make a puppet theatre from furniture and a sheet, or from big cardboard boxes, so you can make up plays for your puppets and moving figures. Try making a film of you theatre.

Ready for more?

- Imagine one of these worlds and draw a picture of it:
  - a world where all the trees are black and people are green
  - a world where everyone has wings
  - a world where dinosaurs are still alive as well as people
  - a world where humans are very small
  - most of the world is water and there are only a few islands to live on, so most people live underwater.

- Now make a scene of your world inside a box. Cut the front out of the box so you can see the scene. Make your picture into the background, and use recycled materials, playdough, small world figures or card cut-outs for the people, animals and scenery. Take some photos of your imagined world and write a story about it.

- Look up these words in Google Images - 'imagined worlds' 'different world' 'landscape' 'moon landscape' 'lunar landscape' 'another world' 'fantasy world'. Use some of the pictures as inspiration for your own pictures, scenes and stories.

- Use the ideas you have worked on to make some fantasy costumes, masks or headgear for a play about a fantasy world. Or have a competition for the best costume or head-dress.

Materials, equipment suppliers, websites, books and other references

Some ideas for **resources and equipment**:

Educational suppliers have small world figures for imaginary worlds, but you may do better on EBay or by asking for cast off figures and play sets that children have grown out of. You could also add some replica minibeasts that can be offered in small containers or baskets to inspire stories and environments - insects, beetles, ants etc.

Some images and websites include:

www.walkerbooks.co.uk have a great selection of their own books about fantasy and imagination sorted by age group and Key Stage.

Try Google Images 'imagined worlds' 'story worlds' 'fantasy worlds' 'other worlds' 'space ship' (Children should always be supervised by an adult when searching in the internet)

www.kid-at-art.com - an art site for children with an 'Imagination Factory' of ideas.

Books and Publications:

Alice's Adventures in Wonderland; Lewis Carrol (illustrated by Helen Oxenbury); Walker Books

It Moved!; An Fine; Walker Books (Lily brings a stone for Show and Tell)

The Book of Beasts; Inga Moore; Walker Books

The Bee-man of Orn; Frank Stockton; Walker Books

The Imagineering Field Guide to the Magic Kingdom at Walt Disney World; Disney Editions

The Bridge to Terrabithia; Catherine Paterson (DVD)

Some books about making masks, face painting and costume making:

I Can Make Costumes; Mary Wallace; Maple Tree Press

The Usborne Book of Face Painting; Chris Caudron; Usborne

Face Painting; Alastair Smith; Usborne

Fantastic Faces Snazaroo; Kingfisher

Starting Face Painting; Fiona Watts; Usborne

Clothes and Shoes; Helen Greathead; Smart Apple Media

Making Masks; Renee Schwarz; Kids Can Press

Watch Me Make a Mask; Jack Otten; Children's Press

How to Make a Mask; by Paul Humphrey; Sea to Sea Publications

Curriculum coverage grid overleaf

Full version of KS1 PoS on pages 69-74
Photocopiable version on page 8

Literacy

	Lit 1 speak	Lit 2 listen	Lit 3 group	Lit 4 drama	Lit 5 word	Lit 6 spell	Lit 7 text1	Lit 8 text2	Lit 9 text3	Lit10 text4	Lit11 sentence	Lit12 presentation
	1.1	2.1	3.1	4.1	5.1	6.1	7.1	8.1	9.1	10.1	11.1	12.1
	1.2	2.2	3.2	4.2	5.2	6.2	7.2	8.2	9.2	10.2	11.2	12.2

Numeracy

	Num 1 U&A	Num 2 count	Num 3 number	Num 4 calculate	Num 5 shape	Num 6 measure	Num 7 data
	1.1	2.1	3.1	4.1	5.1	6.1	7.1
	1.2	2.2	3.2	4.2	5.2	6.2	7.2

Science

SC1 Enquiry			SC2 Life processes					SC3 Materials		SC4 Phys processes		
Sc1.1	Sc1.2	Sc1.3	Sc2.1	Sc2.2	Sc2.3	Sc2.4	Sc2.5	Sc3.1	Sc3.2	Sc4.1	Sc4.2	Sc4.3
1.1a	1.2a	1.3a	2.1a	2.2a	2.3a	2.4a	2.5a	3.1a	3.2a	4.1a	4.2a	4.3a
1.1b	1.2b	1.3b	2.1b	2.2b	2.3b	2.4b	2.5b	3.1b	3.2b	4.1b	4.2b	4.3b
1.1c	1.2c	1.3c	2.1c	2.2c	2.3c		2.5c	3.1c		4.1c	4.2c	4.3c
1.1d				2.2d				3.1d				4.3d
				2.2e								
				2.2f								
				2.2g								

ICT

ICT 1 finding out		ICT 2 ideas	ICT 3 reviewing	ICT 4 breadth
1.1a	1.2a	2a	3a	4a
1.1b	1.2b	2b	3b	4b
1.1c	1.2c	2c	3c	4c
	1.2d			

D&T

D&T 1 developing	D&T 2 tool use	D&T 3 evaluating	D&T 4 materials	D&T 5 breadth
1a	2a	3a	4a	5a
1b	2b	3b	4b	5b
1c	2c			5c
1d	2d			
1e	2e			

History

H1 chronology	H2 events, people	H3 interpret	H4 enquire	H5 org & comm	H6 breadth
1a	2a	3a	4a	5a	6a
1b	2b		4b		6b
					6c
					6d

Geography

G1.1 & G1.2 enquiry		G2 places	G3 processes	G4 environment	G5 breadth
1.1a	1.2a	2a	3a	4a	5a
1.1b	1.2b	2b	3b	4b	5b
1.1c	1.2c	2c			5c
1.1d	1.2d	2d			5d
		2e			

Music

M1 performing	M2 composing	M3 appraising	M4 listening	M5 breadth
1a	2a	3a	4a	5a
1b	2b	3b	4b	5b
1c			4c	5c
				5d

PHSE & C

PSHEC1 conf & resp	PSHEC2 citizenship	PSHEC3 health	PSHEC4 relationships
1a	2a	3a	4a
1b	2b	3b	4b
1c	2c	3c	4c
1d	2d	3d	4d
1e	2e	3e	4e
	2f	3f	
	2g	3g	
	2h		

Art & Design

A&D1 ideas	A&D2 making	A&D3 evaluating	A&D4 materials	A&D5 breadth
1a	2a	3a	4a	5a
1b	2b	3b	4b	5b
	2c		4c	5c
				5d

PE

PE1 devel skills	PE2 apply skills	PE3 evaluate	PE4 fitness	PE5 breadth
1a	2a	3a	4a	5a dance
1b	2b	3b	4b	5b games
	2c	3c		5c gym

Critical skills	Thinking Skills
problem solving	observing
decision making	classifying
critical thinking	prediction
creative thinking	making inferences
communication	problem solving
organisation	drawing conclusions
management	
leadership	

Treasure Boxes

Treasure Boxes

Previous experience in the Foundation Stage
Most children will have worked with a wide range of artefacts in a variety of contexts through:
* free play indoors and outside;
* story sacks and boxes;
* collecting and 'treasure bags', both personal and setting based;
* home corner and imaginative play;
* prop boxes;

They will have experienced:
* a wide range of stories;
* stories on audio tape, videotape, film and DVD;
* computer games.

All these experiences will have developed their imagination and equipped them for many of the challenges that can be offered through Treasure Boxes.

Pause for thought
In the early stages of working with these materials it is crucial to continue to observe the children. Only by doing this can you set developmentally appropriate challenges and provocations. The ideas listed here are offered as suggestions; the most exciting challenges will arise from children's own interests and motivations, which will only become apparent as you spend time with them, watching and joining them in their play. As you do this, you will be moving between the three interconnecting roles of observer, co-player, extender described below, and will be able to decide what you need to do next to take the learning forward.

The responsive adult (see page 5)
In three interconnecting roles, the responsive adult will be:

* observing
* listening
* interpreting

observer

* **modelling**
* **playing alongside**
* **offering suggestions**
* **responding sensitively**
* **initiating with care!**

co-player

* discussing ideas
* sharing thinking
* modelling new skills
* asking open questions
* being an informed extender
* instigating ideas & thoughts
* supporting children as they make links in learning
* making possibilities evident
* introducing new ideas and resources
* offering challenges and provocations

extender

Offering challenges and provocations - some ideas:
Provide children with plenty of different sorts of containers for collections and treasures. They don't need to be expensive - gift boxes and bags, cotton carriers and shopping bags, packaging from cosmetics and jewellery, chocolate boxes, biscuit tins etc. will all be appreciated.

? Find a treasure box or bag and fill it with objects. Now list all the objects in your box in alphabetical order. Take photos and describe each one.

? Choose a box and collect some treasures from the garden of your school (nice stones, leaves, flowers etc). Now give the box to a friend and let them make up a story about the things you collected.

? Work with some friends. Choose a box each and put five things in your own box. Make the objects as interesting as you can. Exchange boxes with one of your friends and decide who the box belongs to. Give a name to your character and tell the group what the character does with each of the things in the box.

? Bring three unusual small things from home (ones that belong to you or have been given to you). Put all the objects in a bag and take turns choosing one with your eyes closed and saying what it is and the character it could belong to.

? Can you make and decorate a treasure box? Use recycled materials or a ready made box as a base, and find some objects to decorate it with. Then fill your box with treasure and make up a story or play to go with it. You could make up a rap or song to go with the story.

? Google 'make a treasure chest' to find some great instructions and ideas or Google Images 'treasure chest' for pictures of chests and ideas for decorating them. You could follow some of these instructions and make a really exciting chest for a play or just a game.

Ready for more?

- Look on the Internet or in the library for books about treasure, treasure boxes and hidden treasure. If you search www.amazon.co.uk for 'treasure' and then search children's books, you'll find a lot of stories about treasures.

- Make a message chest, where you can leave messages for your friends to find. These could be clues or instructions of where to find something you have hidden.

- Make a board game or race game about hidden treasure. It could be a pirate game, Ancient Egypt, or an adventure game. The game could be made with chalk on the playground or on a board for indoor play.

- Make up your own treasure box and make a treasure hunt to go with it. Write a story about your treasure hunt.

- Work with some friends to make some photos of places in your school and in the playground, grounds and gardens. Use these photos to make up a story about a hidden treasure in your school. You could make a book with the photos and some more taken as you play out the story.

- Find a copy of Treasure Island by Robert Louis Stevenson. Read some of the story, then act it out. It's a long story so you could ask your teacher to read it to your class in chapters, then act out each chapter after you have listened to it.

Materials, equipment suppliers, websites, books and other references

Suppliers of equipment and resources:

Keep your eye open for:

- bargain boxes and containers in charity shops and other bargain shops. You can sometimes find really unusual boxes and other containers. A spray with gold or silver aerosol paint will make even ordinary objects look like treasure, or children could wrap them in kitchen foil.
- foreign or old coins. Many people still have coins or even notes from holidays in countries where they now use Euros.
- jewellery, beads, old brooches, shiny pebbles, glass 'beads' can all become treasure to collect, bury and find again.

Try **Google** to find out about jewels and treasure.

www.ukoln.ac.uk - and click through to find Treasure Island for things to make, games and challenges;

www.britishcouncil.org/kids-stories-treasure-map - for a treasure map and story;

www.crawler.com - then 'treasure map for kids' will get you to lots of downloadable treasure maps and ideas including a treasure collection set in jelly. www.ukoln.ac.uk - and click through to find Treasure Island for things to make, games and challenges. www.nationalgeographic.com/pirates - also about pirates, with lots of books and other information. www.piratesinfo.com - just about pirates!

Google Images 'treasure map' 'treasure chest' 'treasure island' 'pirates'

The Little Book of Treasure Boxes (from www.featherstone.uk.com) has ideas for collections.

Some Books

The Treasure Hunt (Tales from Percy's Park); Nick Butterworth; Picture Lions

Treasure Sock; Pat Thompson; Puffin

Rare Treasure: Mary Anning and Her Remarkable Discoveries; Don Brown; Houghton Mifflin

Stone Girl Bone Girl: The Story of Mary Anning; Laurence Anholt; Frances Lincoln

The Fossil Girl (Paperback); Katherine Brighton; Houghton Mifflin

Pirate Pink and Treasures of the Reef; Jan Day; Pelican

Buried Treasure (Barkley's School for Dogs); Marcia Jones; Hyperion

The Treasure Hunt; Nick Butterworth; Picture Lions

Treasure Hunts! Treasure Hunts!; Lenny Hort; HarperCollins

Mrs Pepperpot and the Hidden Treasure; Alf Proysen; Red Fox

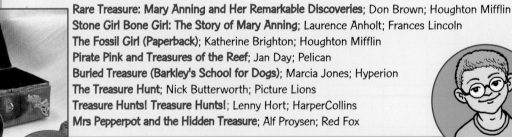

Curriculum coverage grid overleaf

Potential NC KS1 Curriculum Coverage through the provocations suggested for treasure boxes

Literacy

	Lit 1 speak	Lit 2 listen	Lit 3 group	Lit 4 drama	Lit 5 word	Lit 6 spell	Lit 7 text1	Lit 8 text2	Lit 9 text3	Lit10 text4	Lit11 sentence	Lit12 presentation
Literacy	1.1	2.1	3.1	4.1	5.1	6.1	7.1	8.1	9.1	10.1	11.1	12.1
	1.2	2.2	3.2	4.2	5.2	6.2	7.2	8.2	9.2	10.2	11.2	12.2

Numeracy

	Num 1 U&A	Num 2 count	Num 3 number	Num 4 calculate	Num 5 shape	Num 6 measure	Num 7 data
Numeracy	1.1	2.1	3.1	4.1	5.1	6.1	7.1
	1.2	2.2	3.2	4.2	5.2	6.2	7.2

Full version of KS1 PoS on pages 69-74
Photocopiable version on page 8

Science

	SC1 Enquiry			SC2 Life processes					SC3 Materials		SC4 Phys processes		
	Sc1.1	Sc1.2	Sc1.3	Sc2.1	Sc2.2	Sc2.3	Sc2.4	Sc2.5	Sc3.1	Sc3.2	Sc4.1	Sc4.2	Sc4.3
Science	1.1a	1.2a	1.3a	2.1a	2.2a	2.3a	2.4a	2.5a	3.1a	3.2a	4.1a	4.2a	4.3a
	1.1b	1.2b	1.3b	2.1b	2.2b	2.3b	2.4b	2.5b	3.1b	3.2b	4.1b	4.2b	4.3b
	1.1c	1.2c	1.3c	2.1c	2.2c	2.3c		2.5c	3.1c		4.1c	4.2c	4.3c
	1.1d				2.2d				3.1d				4.3d
					2.2e								
					2.2f								
					2.2g								

ICT

	ICT 1 finding out		ICT 2 ideas	ICT 3 reviewing	ICT 4 breadth
ICT	1.1a	1.2a	2a	3a	4a
	1.1b	1.2b	2b	3b	4b
	1.1c	1.2c	2c	3c	4c
		1.2d			

D&T

	D&T 1 developing	D&T 2 tool use	D&T 3 evaluating	D&T 4 materials	D&T 5 breadth
D&T	1a	2a	3a	4a	5a
	1b	2b	3b	4b	5b
	1c	2c			5c
	1d	2d			
	1e	2e			

History

	H1 chronology	H2 events, people	H3 interpret	H4 enquire	H5 org & comm	H6 breadth
History	1a	2a	3a	4a	5a	6a
	1b	2b		4b		6b
						6c
						6d

Geography

	G1.1 & G1.2 enquiry		G2 places	G3 processes	G4 environment	G5 breadth
Geography	1.1a	1.2a	2a	3a	4a	5a
	1.1b	1.2b	2b	3b	4b	5b
	1.1c	1.2c	2c			5c
	1.1d	1.2d	2d			5d
			2e			

Music

	M1 performing	M2 composing	M3 appraising	M4 listening	M5 breadth
Music	1a	2a	3a	4a	5a
	1b	2b	3b	4b	5b
	1c			4c	5c
					5d

PSHE & C

	PSHEC1 conf & resp	PSHEC2 citizenship	PSHEC3 health	PSHEC4 relationships
PHSE & C	1a	2a	3a	4a
	1b	2b	3b	4b
	1c	2c	3c	4c
	1d	2d	3d	4d
	1e	2e	3e	4e
		2f	3f	
		2g	3g	
		2h		

Art & Design

	A&D1 ideas	A&D2 making	A&D3 evaluating	A&D4 materials	A&D5 breadth
Art & Design	1a	2a	3a	4a	5a
	1b	2b	3b	4b	5b
		2c		4c	5c
					5d

PE

	PE1 devel skills	PE2 apply skills	PE3 evaluate	PE4 fitness	PE5 breadth
PE	1a	2a	3a	4a	5a dance
	1b	2b	3b	4b	5b games
		2c	3c		5c gym

Critical skills / Thinking Skills

Critical skills	Thinking Skills
problem solving	observing
decision making	classifying
critical thinking	prediction
creative thinking	making inferences
communication	problem solving
organisation	drawing conclusions
management	
leadership	

Houses and Homes

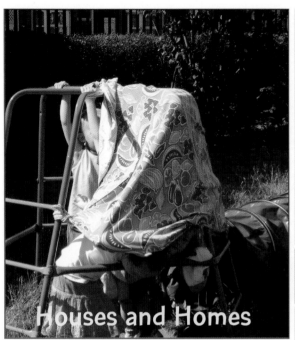

Houses and Homes

Previous experience in the Foundation Stage
Throughout the early years, children will have been making homes and playing in them. Family and home role play is a favourite activity for all children, both indoors and outside, and every child will be familiar with this sort of play:

* in home corner play;
* when making dens and shelters;
* in play in tents, gazebos and other temporary constructions;
* through picnics and eating out of doors;
* in role play camping;
* using doll's houses and small world people;
* playing with soft toys and puppets;
* making and playing with play food, tea-sets, baskets and boxes.

Pause for thought
In the early stages of working with these materials it is crucial to continue to observe the children. Only by doing this can you set developmentally appropriate challenges and provocations. The ideas listed here are offered as suggestions; the most exciting challenges will arise from children's own interests and motivations, which will only become apparent as you spend time with them, watching and joining them in their play. As you do this, you will be moving between the three interconnecting roles of observer, co-player, extender described below, and will be able to decide what you need to do next to take the learning forward.

The responsive adult (see page 5)

In three interconnecting roles, the responsive adult will be:

* observing
* listening
* interpreting

observer

* **modelling**
* **playing alongside**
* **offering suggestions**
* **responding sensitively**
* **initiating with care!**

co-player

* discussing ideas
* sharing thinking
* modelling new skills
* asking open questions
* being an informed extender
* instigating ideas & thoughts
* supporting children as they make links in learning
* making possibilities evident
* introducing new ideas and resources
* offering challenges and provocations

extender

Offering challenges and provocations - some ideas:

NOTE: Providing ongoing opportunities for home play will help children to continue playing out the experiences they have at home and in their communities. However, there will be many opportunities to offer house and home play connected with topics, themes and subjects of the curriculum:

? Possibilities for curriculum related house and home play might include:
  * homes from other times, such as a castle, a Victorian kitchen, a prehistoric cave;
  * homes from other places, such as an African, Indian or Chinese home, a tepee or igloo;
  * homes from stories, such as Hogwarts or Sleeping Beauty's Castle;
  * animal homes, such as a pond, a bear's lair, a cave or a nest;
  * different places to live, such as a lighthouse, a caravan, a pirate ship.

? Can you use recycled materials, canes and cable ties to make a den or shelter in the outdoor area? Make your den comfortable and use it as a place to play and talk.

? Can you use pegs and fabrics to make a shelter by pegging the fabric to a fence or railings? Make a notice for your den, so other children know what the den is for.

? Can you make a house for some small world people, using recycled materials such as boxes and scraps of fabric. Dress the people and make up a story about what they do in the house. take some photos or make a video.

? See if you can borrow a pop-up tent. Turn the tent into one of these places:
  * a space station
  * post office
  * a home for some Hobbits

Decorate the inside and outside so everyone knows what sort of house it is.

Ready for more?

- Find some cardboard boxes, tubes and other recycled materials. Can you make these into a castle? Is the castle big enough for you to get inside?

- Look up 'dolls house' in Google Images. Now can you work with some friends to make a dolls house of your own. It could be for:
  - small dolls
  - a superhero
  - a story character
  - or anyone else

  Use recycled materials and scraps of patterned paper or fabric to make furnishings and clothing for the people who live in the house you have made.

- Collect some twigs, sticks, leaves, grass, hay and other natural materials and make a home for some small world animals. Use books or the internet to find out what sort of home each animal needs.

- Work with some friends to use fabrics or dressing up clothes to turn yourselves into new characters. When you have done this, make some props, masks or jewellery, so you can really turn into the characters. Find or make some face paints so you can decorate yourselves. Practice walking, sitting, eating and talking like your new character.

- Find a camera and use it to photograph each other in your new characters. Make the photos into a photo book or powerpoint presentation.

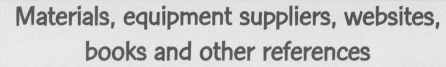

Materials, equipment suppliers, websites, books and other references

Try www.communityplaythings.co.uk or www.ed-solutionsdirect.coms.co.uk or http://woodentotsmk.co.uk for role play equipment and furniture;
www.threebearsplaythings.co.uk - have play screens
www.argos.co.uk for cheap tea-sets and www.amazon.co.uk for cheap plastic food and other role play equipment;
www.jellydeal.co.uk have some good deals on workbenches, kitchens, cash registers, and a 120 piece play food set;
www.mindstretchers.co.uk - have den building kits, shade sails, waterproof sheets and willow structures;
and at www.domesticproduct.co.uk for a prizewinning design for a willow playhouse.
Look at the Year 1 part of this site www.christchurchcofeschool.co.uk to see their projects
Try **Google** Images: 'doll's house' 'house' 'tent' 'shelter'.

Some Books about houses and homes:

Houses and Homes: Ann Morris; William Morrow
The Village of Round and Square Houses: Ann Grifalconi; Macmillan
The Dolls' House; Rumer Godden; Macmillan
Toby's Doll's House; Ragnhild Scamell; Gullane Children's Books
Miss Brick the Builder's Baby; Allan Ahlberg; Puffin
Doll's House; Adele Geras; Longman
Connor's Eco Den; Pippa Goodhart; Barrington Stoke
The Best Den Ever; A Cassidy; Franklin Watts
Wizard's Den: Spellbinding Stories of Magic and Magicians; Peter Haining; Souvenir Press
Tepee; Dana Meachen Rau; Benchmark
The Little Book of Outdoor Play; A & C Black
See Inside Castles; Katie Daynes; Usborne
The Story of Castles; Lesley Simms; Usborne
Castles; Peter D Riley; Scholastic
Arthur Goes to Camp; Marc Tolon Brown; Little Brown
Camp Out!: The Ultimate Kids' Guide; Lynn Brunelle; Scholastic

Curriculum coverage grid overleaf

Potential NC KS1 Curriculum Coverage through the provocations suggested for houses and homes

Full version of KS1 PoS on pages 69-74
Photocopiable version on page 8

Literacy

	Lit 1 speak	Lit 2 listen	Lit 3 group	Lit 4 drama	Lit 5 word	Lit 6 spell	Lit 7 text1	Lit 8 text2	Lit 9 text3	Lit10 text4	Lit11 sen-tence	Lit12 present-ation
Literacy	1.1	2.1	3.1	4.1	5.1	6.1	7.1	8.1	9.1	10.1	11.1	12.1
	1.2	2.2	3.2	4.2	5.2	6.2	7.2	8.2	9.2	10.2	11.2	12.2

Numeracy

	Num 1 U&A	Num 2 count	Num 3 number	Num 4 calculate	Num 5 shape	Num 6 measure	Num 7 data
Numeracy	1.1	2.1	3.1	4.1	5.1	6.1	7.1
	1.2	2.2	3.2	4.2	5.2	6.2	7.2

Science

	SC1 Enquiry			SC2 Life processes					SC3 Materials		SC4 Phys processes		
	Sc1.1	Sc1.2	Sc1.3	Sc2.1	Sc2.2	Sc2.3	Sc2.4	Sc2.5	Sc3.1	Sc3.2	Sc4.1	Sc4.2	Sc4.3
	1.1a	1.2a	1.3a	2.1a	2.2a	2.3a	2.4a	2.5a	3.1a	3.2a	4.1a	4.2a	4.3a
Science	1.1b	1.2b	1.3b	2.1b	2.2b	2.3b	2.4b	2.5b	3.1b	3.2b	4.1b	4.2b	4.3b
	1.1c	1.2c	1.3c	2.1c	2.2c	2.3c		2.5c	3.1c		4.1c	4.2c	4.3c
	1.1d				2.2d				3.1d				4.3d
					2.2e								
					2.2f								
					2.2g								

ICT

	ICT 1 finding out	ICT 2 ideas	ICT 3 reviewing	ICT 4 breadth
	1.1a	1.2a	2a	3a	4a
ICT	1.1b	1.2b	2b	3b	4b
	1.1c	1.2c	2c	3c	4c
		1.2d			

D&T

	D&T 1 developing	D&T 2 tool use	D&T 3 evaluating	D&T 4 materials	D&T 5 breadth
	1a	2a	3a	4a	5a
D&T	1b	2b	3b	4b	5b
	1c	2c			5c
	1d	2d			
	1e	2e			

History

	H1 chron-ology	H2 events, people	H3 inter-pret	H4 enquire	H5 org & comm	H6 breadth
	1a	2a	3a	4a	5a	6a
History	1b	2b		4b		6b
						6c
						6d

Geography

	G1.1 & G1.2 enquiry		G2 places	G3 processes	G4 environment	G5 breadth
	1.1a	1.2a	2a	3a	4a	5a
Geog-raphy	1.1b	1.2b	2b	3b	4b	5b
	1.1c	1.2c	2c			5c
	1.1d	1.2d	2d			5d
			2e			

Music

	M1 performing	M2 composing	M3 appraising	M4 listening	M5 breadth
	1a	2a	3a	4a	5a
Music	1b	2b	3b	4b	5b
	1c			4c	5c
					5d

PHSE & C

	PSHEC1 conf & resp	PSHEC2 citizenship	PSHEC3 health	PSHEC4 relationships
	1a	2a	3a	4a
	1b	2b	3b	4b
PHSE & C	1c	2c	3c	4c
	1d	2d	3d	4d
	1e	2e	3e	4e
		2f	3f	
		2g	3g	
		2h		

Art & Design

	A&D1 ideas	A&D2 making	A&D3 evaluating	A&D4 materials	A&D5 breadth
	1a	2a	3a	4a	5a
Art & Design	1b	2b	3b	4b	5b
		2c		4c	5c
					5d

PE

	PE1 devel skills	PE2 apply skills	PE3 evaluate	PE4 fitness	PE5 breadth
	1a	2a	3a	4a	5a dance
PE	1b	2b	3b	4b	5b games
		2c	3c		5c gym

Critical skills	Thinking Skills
problem solving	observing
decision making	classifying
critical thinking	prediction
creative thinking	making inferences
communication	problem solving
organisation	drawing conclusions
management	
leadership	

Puppets and Moving Objects

Puppets

Previous experience in the Foundation Stage

Puppets are familiar resources in the Foundation Stage, and most children will have:

* played with finger puppets;
* used hand or glove puppets freely and in story telling or numeracy sessions;
* experienced adults using larger 'people puppets' for work on feelings and during circle time;
* made puppet shows to tell their own stories or re-tell those they have heard;
* used puppets during literacy sessions;

they may also have made puppets from

* recycled materials, felt, fabric etc;
* card, using paper fasteners and string to make moving figures.

Pause for thought

In the early stages of working with these materials it is crucial to continue to observe the children. Only by doing this can you set developmentally appropriate challenges and provocations. The ideas listed here are offered as suggestions; the most exciting challenges will arise from children's own interests and motivations, which will only become apparent as you spend time with them, watching and joining them in their play. As you do this, you will be moving between the three interconnecting roles of observer, co-player, extender described below, and will be able to decide what you need to do next to take the learning forward.

The responsive adult (see page 5)

In three interconnecting roles, the responsive adult will be:

* observing
* listening
* interpreting

observer

* modelling
* playing alongside
* offering suggestions
* responding sensitively
* initiating with care!

co-player

* discussing ideas
* sharing thinking
* modelling new skills
* asking open questions
* being an informed extender
* instigating ideas & thoughts
* supporting children as they make links in learning
* making possibilities evident
* introducing new ideas and resources
* offering challenges and provocations

extender

Offering challenges and provocations - some ideas:

NOTE: Offer all sorts of den building materials to the children - canes, sticks, fabrics (lightweight ones are easiest to manage), clips and pegs, string and rope, boxes and cardboard.

? Can you make a puppet from one of these things:
* a sock?
* a paper bag?
* a carrier bag?
* a glove?

Now decorate your puppet with anything you like.

? Find a big cardboard box and work with a friend to turn it into a puppet theatre. Use the theatre for puppet plays using the puppets you have made.

? Can you make a moving figure from card and paper fasteners? (look on Google at 'card puppet' or 'rod puppet' for some ideas) You could make:
* a robot
* a pecking bird
* a dinosaur or crocodile with big teeth
* a walking person.

? Use a puppet theatre to show how your puppets work.

? Choose a number song or rhyme, then work with some friends to make finger puppets to make the counting rhyme more interesting. You could use the fingers of an old pair of gloves to make the puppets, and decorate them with paper or felt.

? Find some magazines and use the pictures to make puppets. Cut out people and animals, stick them on card and then stick the card on a lolly stick or a plastic straw. You could make pop star puppets, football puppets, or animal ones. Use your puppets to make up stories, play games or dance to music.

Ready for more?

- Put 'string puppet' or 'rod puppet' in Google Images. Use the pictures to see if you can find some instructions for making string or rod puppets. Use the instructions to make some puppets of your own.

- Choose a story or a film that you really like. Now make some puppets of the characters, draw or paint a background and make up a puppet play.

- Find some old gloves with fingers. Now make a hand puppet by sticking a face on each finger. Use these puppets to tell stories. You could go to Reception and do a play for them.

- Try making a life sized puppet that you can work by fixing their feet to your feet and their hands to your hands. You will probably need a friend to help you! You could use real clothes and shoes, and some gloves.

- Use the internet to find out how to make papier mache puppet heads. Put 'papier mache puppets' in Google and see what you can find. You may be able to print off some instructions. Now try making some of these puppets yourselves.

- Make some puppets of your friends. Take a photo of your friend's head and shoulders. Print the photo, and either cut it out and stick it on card, or stick it on the head of a glove puppet or stick puppet.

Materials, equipment suppliers, websites, books and other references

Children need lots of resources to make puppets and moving objects for their play, and many of these are cheap or even free. Try collecting some of these:
- sticks and canes;
- cable ties, string, tape of all sorts;
- paper clips and fasteners, pegs, clips, elastic, hair 'scrunchies';
- card, stiff paper, plastic, bubble wrap;
- plastic carrier bags and bin bags;
- cardboard boxes;
- cardboard sheeting from the sides of boxes and cartons.

Some useful websites

www.puppetsbypost.com for a huge selection of puppets of all sizes and types;
www.ascoeducational.co.uk for empathy dolls, small world figures and vehicles;
http://woodfield.ethink.org.uk/2008 (a school site) and look at their pop-up-puppets;
www.auntannie.com/puppets.html is an electronic book of crafts including puppets;
www.enchantedlearning.com/crafts/puppets for ideas and instructions;
www.vam.ac.uk is a site where you can download clips of moving toys;
www.standards.dfes.gov.uk/schemes2 is a government contact for a KS1 curriculum topic on moving toys.

Google Images 'string puppet' 'glove puppet' 'finger puppet' 'puppet theatre' 'moving toy'.

Books and Stories:

Creative Art Puppets (Creative Art and Activities) (Paperback) ; Mayesky; Delmar Learning
Make Your Own Puppets and Puppet Theaters: Williamson
How to Make Puppets with Children; Joy Evans; Evan-Moore
Easy-to-make Puppets and How to Use Them; Fran Rottman; Regal Books
How to Make Animated Toys; David Wakefield; Sterling
Easy-to-make Old Fashioned Toys; Eugene Privenzo; Dover
Make Toys; Diane James; Two-Can
Toys That Move; Helen Greathead; Smart Apple Media
Puppets; Susie Hodge; Smart Apple Media
The Little Book of Puppet Making; Suzy Tutchell; Featherstone Education
How To Make a Scarecrow; Kim Wilde; Collins Big Cat

Curriculum coverage grid overleaf

Potential NC KS1 Curriculum Coverage through the provocations suggested for puppets and moving objects.

Full version of KS1 PoS on pages 69-74
Photocopiable version on page 8

Literacy

Lit 1 speak	Lit 2 listen	Lit 3 group	Lit 4 drama	Lit 5 word	Lit 6 spell	Lit 7 text1	Lit 8 text2	Lit 9 text3	Lit10 text4	Lit11 sentence	Lit12 presentation
1.1	2.1	3.1	4.1	5.1	6.1	7.1	8.1	9.1	10.1	11.1	12.1
1.2	2.2	3.2	4.2	5.2	6.2	7.2	8.2	9.2	10.2	11.2	12.2

Numeracy

Num 1 U&A	Num 2 count	Num 3 number	Num 4 calculate	Num 5 shape	Num 6 measure	Num 7 data
1.1	2.1	3.1	4.1	5.1	6.1	7.1
1.2	2.2	3.2	4.2	5.2	6.2	7.2

Science

SC1 Enquiry			SC2 Life processes					SC3 Materials		SC4 Phys processes		
Sc1.1	Sc1.2	Sc1.3	Sc2.1	Sc2.2	Sc2.3	Sc2.4	Sc2.5	Sc3.1	Sc3.2	Sc4.1	Sc4.2	Sc4.3
1.1a	1.2a	1.3a	2.1a	2.2a	2.3a	2.4a	2.5a	3.1a	3.2a	4.1a	4.2a	4.3a
1.1b	1.2b	1.3b	2.1b	2.2b	2.3b	2.4b	2.5b	3.1b	3.2b	4.1b	4.2b	4.3b
1.1c	1.2c	1.3c	2.1c	2.2c	2.3c		2.5c	3.1c		4.1c	4.2c	4.3c
1.1d				2.2d				3.1d				4.3d
				2.2e								
				2.2f								
				2.2g								

ICT

ICT 1 finding out		ICT 2 ideas	ICT 3 reviewing	ICT 4 breadth
1.1a	1.2a	2a	3a	4a
1.1b	1.2b	2b	3b	4b
1.1c	1.2c	2c	3c	4c
	1.2d			

D&T

D&T 1 developing	D&T 2 tool use	D&T 3 evaluating	D&T 4 materials	D&T 5 breadth
1a	2a	3a	4a	5a
1b	2b	3b	4b	5b
1c	2c			5c
1d	2d			
1e	2e			

History

H1 chronology	H2 events, people	H3 interpret	H4 enquire	H5 org & comm	H6 breadth
1a	2a	3a	4a	5a	6a
1b	2b		4b		6b
					6c
					6d

Geography

G1.1 & G1.2 enquiry		G2 places	G3 processes	G4 environment	G5 breadth
1.1a	1.2a	2a	3a	4a	5a
1.1b	1.2b	2b	3b	4b	5b
1.1c	1.2c	2c			5c
1.1d	1.2d	2d			5d
		2e			

Music

M1 performing	M2 composing	M3 appraising	M4 listening	M5 breadth
1a	2a	3a	4a	5a
1b	2b	3b	4b	5b
1c			4c	5c
				5d

PHSE & C

PSHEC1 conf & resp	PSHEC2 citizenship	PSHEC3 health	PSHEC4 relationships
1a	2a	3a	4a
1b	2b	3b	4b
1c	2c	3c	4c
1d	2d	3d	4d
1e	2e	3e	4e
	2f	3f	
	2g	3g	
	2h		

Art & Design

A&D1 ideas	A&D2 making	A&D3 evaluating	A&D4 materials	A&D5 breadth
1a	2a	3a	4a	5a
1b	2b	3b	4b	5b
	2c		4c	5c
				5d

PE

PE1 devel skills	PE2 apply skills	PE3 evaluate	PE4 fitness	PE5 breadth
1a	2a	3a	4a	5a dance
1b	2b	3b	4b	5b games
	2c	3c		5c gym

Critical skills	Thinking Skills
problem solving	observing
decision making	classifying
critical thinking	prediction
creative thinking	making inferences
communication	problem solving
organisation	drawing conclusions
management	
leadership	

Small Worlds

Small Worlds

Previous experience in the Foundation Stage

Children will certainly have played with small world figures, people and animals of all sorts and scales. These may have included:

* zoo, farm and other sorts of animals;
* play people from construction sets - Lego, Playmobil, Sticklebricks etc;
* TV and video characters;
* story characters;
* space and adventure figures;
* superheroes, knights, dragons;
* small dolls such as Barbie, Polly Pocket, Sindy, Dora the Explorer;

They may also have made

* props for the small world figures;
* settings, houses and environments for the figures.

Pause for thought

In the early stages of working with these materials it is crucial to continue to observe the children. Only by doing this can you set developmentally appropriate challenges and provocations. The ideas listed here are offered as suggestions; the most exciting challenges will arise from children's own interests and motivations, which will only become apparent as you spend time with them, watching and joining them in their play. As you do this, you will be moving between the three interconnecting roles of observer, co-player, extender described below, and will be able to decide what you need to do next to take the learning forward.

The responsive adult (see page 5)

In three interconnecting roles, the responsive adult will be:

observer

* observing
* listening
* interpreting

co-player

* modelling
* playing alongside
* offering suggestions
* responding sensitively
* initiating with care!

extender

* discussing ideas
* sharing thinking
* modelling new skills
* asking open questions
* being an informed extender
* instigating ideas & thoughts
* supporting children as they make links in learning
* making possibilities evident
* introducing new ideas and resources
* offering challenges and provocations

Offering challenges and provocations - some ideas:

NOTE: Small world play offers many of the experiences of whole bode role play, while taking up less space, and needing less preparation. Some children also find it more engaging. Offering opportunities to use the mall world figures children enjoy at home can be a good basis for story telling and literacy and topic work.

? Find some small world animals and make an environment for them. You could make:
  * a safari park
  * a farm
  * a jungle
  * an arctic scene
  * a desert

Use a tray, shallow box or 'builder's tray' as a base, then add sticks, leaves, stones, grass, gravel, sand and other things to make the environment. Photograph your work.

? Now add some people to your setting and play out some adventures. Take a series of photos of the adventure.

? Can you make a house for some small world people? You could choose the people, and use some from school or bring some from home. Find some recycled or natural materials, and some fabrics to make the house comfortable, interesting and suitable for the characters.

? Could you make one of these:
  * a hammock for a superhero?
  * a wardrobe for Barbie's clothes?
  * a rocket or spaceship for small world spacemen?
  * an assault course for some explorer figures?
  * a cartoon house for some cartoon characters?
  * a stage for a show by some TV characters?

Ready for more?

- Can you make a film or photo sequence of a story where the characters are small world people?
- Take some small world people outside and take some photos of them:
  - in long grass, on branches
  - in bushes
  - under leaves
  - in holes in the ground.

  Then put your photos together and add a story line to make a photo story book or powerpoint presentation
- Put 'superhero toy' 'character toy' 'film character toy' 'Disney toy' 'harry potter toy' or 'Barbie toy' in Google images. Use some of the images to help you make up a story or draw scenery for action settings for your own toys.
- Can you make a castle for fantasy characters, or knights and dragons. Use recycled materials, such as boxes, tubes from snacks or sweets, polystyrene, offcuts of wood etc. When it is finished, you could use the castle for games, stories or films.
- Find as many wooden or plastic bricks as you can and work as a group to make a huge environment for all the small world characters you can. Make different bits for different groups of figures, fields and woods for animals, towers for princesses, courtyards for knights, lairs for villains. Now work together to make up stories where the different groups of characters meet each other. What happens?

Materials, equipment suppliers, websites, books and other references

Small world figures, play mats and tuff spot scenes are readily available from educational suppliers. It's wise to buy the best quality figures you can afford, as they are more realistic, last longer and they will stand up!

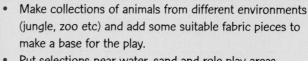

- Make collections of animals from different environments (jungle, zoo etc) and add some suitable fabric pieces to make a base for the play.
- Put selections near water, sand and role play areas.
- Add small world figures to story bags and collections for playing out children's own stories or favourite story books.
- Make some play bases with papier mache or Modroc plaster bandage to stimulate play. Buy or make some play mats - use carpet offcuts and paint on them with a mixture of paint and PVA glue.
- Encourage play with small world vehicles and play people, including fantasy sets such as knights or dragons.
- Use compost, sand, gravel, logs, pebbles, stones or shavings in tuff spot trays to inspire environment building.

Add some non-fiction books and a range of natural materials to small world collections to encourage play and the making of appropriate environments.

Try **Google Images** 'small world' or 'plastic animals' 'toy farm animals' 'play mat' 'airport play mat' 'dinosaur play mat' 'underwater play mat' 'tuff spot' 'toy stable' 'toy farm' 'toy castle' 'toy space station'

or for ideas of landscapes for backgrounds or play mats try 'toy landscape' 'future landscape' 'fantasy landscape' 'fairy landscape'.

Some books:

Minibeasts; Rachel Sparks-Linfield; A & C Black
The Bugliest Bug; Carol Diggory Shields; HarperCollins
Some Smug Slug; Pamela Duncan Edwards; Gibbs Smith
Animals and the Environment; Jennifer Boothroyd; Lerner Publications

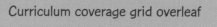
Curriculum coverage grid overleaf

Potential NC KS1 Curriculum Coverage through the provocations suggested for small worlds

Literacy

	Lit 1 speak	Lit 2 listen	Lit 3 group	Lit 4 drama	Lit 5 word	Lit 6 spell	Lit 7 text1	Lit 8 text2	Lit 9 text3	Lit10 text4	Lit11 sentence	Lit12 presentation
Literacy	1.1	2.1	3.1	4.1	5.1	6.1	7.1	8.1	9.1	10.1	11.1	12.1
	1.2	2.2	3.2	4.2	5.2	6.2	7.2	8.2	9.2	10.2	11.2	12.2

Numeracy

	Num 1 U&A	Num 2 count	Num 3 number	Num 4 calculate	Num 5 shape	Num 6 measure	Num 7 data
Numeracy	1.1	2.1	3.1	4.1	5.1	6.1	7.1
	1.2	2.2	3.2	4.2	5.2	6.2	7.2

Full version of KS1 PoS on pages 69-74
Photocopiable version on page 8

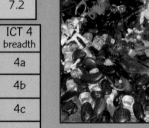

Science

	SC1 Enquiry			SC2 Life processes					SC3 Materials		SC4 Phys processes		
	Sc1.1	Sc1.2	Sc1.3	Sc2.1	Sc2.2	Sc2.3	Sc2.4	Sc2.5	Sc3.1	Sc3.2	Sc4.1	Sc4.2	Sc4.3
Science	1.1a	1.2a	1.3a	2.1a	2.2a	2.3a	2.4a	2.5a	3.1a	3.2a	4.1a	4.2a	4.3a
	1.1b	1.2b	1.3b	2.1b	2.2b	2.3b	2.4b	2.5b	3.1b	3.2b	4.1b	4.2b	4.3b
	1.1c	1.2c	1.3c	2.1c	2.2c	2.3c		2.5c	3.1c		4.1c	4.2c	4.3c
	1.1d				2.2d				3.1d				4.3d
					2.2e								
					2.2f								
					2.2g								

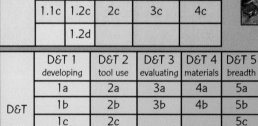

ICT

	ICT 1 finding out		ICT 2 ideas	ICT 3 reviewing	ICT 4 breadth
ICT	1.1a	1.2a	2a	3a	4a
	1.1b	1.2b	2b	3b	4b
	1.1c	1.2c	2c	3c	4c
		1.2d			

D&T

	D&T 1 developing	D&T 2 tool use	D&T 3 evaluating	D&T 4 materials	D&T 5 breadth
D&T	1a	2a	3a	4a	5a
	1b	2b	3b	4b	5b
	1c	2c			5c
	1d	2d			
	1e	2e			

History

	H1 chronology	H2 events, people	H3 interpret	H4 enquire	H5 org & comm	H6 breadth
History	1a	2a	3a	4a	5a	6a
	1b	2b		4b		6b
						6c
						6d

Geography

	G1.1 & G1.2 enquiry		G2 places	G3 processes	G4 environment	G5 breadth
Geography	1.1a	1.2a	2a	3a	4a	5a
	1.1b	1.2b	2b	3b	4b	5b
	1.1c	1.2c	2c			5c
	1.1d	1.2d	2d			5d
			2e			

Music

	M1 performing	M2 composing	M3 appraising	M4 listening	M5 breadth
Music	1a	2a	3a	4a	5a
	1b	2b	3b	4b	5b
	1c			4c	5c
					5d

PHSE & C

	PSHEC1 conf & resp	PSHEC2 citizenship	PSHEC3 health	PSHEC4 relationships
PHSE & C	1a	2a	3a	4a
	1b	2b	3b	4b
	1c	2c	3c	4c
	1d	2d	3d	4d
	1e	2e	3e	4e
		2f	3f	
		2g	3g	
		2h		

Art & Design

	A&D1 ideas	A&D2 making	A&D3 evaluating	A&D4 materials	A&D5 breadth
Art & Design	1a	2a	3a	4a	5a
	1b	2b	3b	4b	5b
		2c		4c	5c
					5d

PE

	PE1 devel skills	PE2 apply skills	PE3 evaluate	PE4 fitness	PE5 breadth
PE	1a	2a	3a	4a	5a dance
	1b	2b	3b	4b	5b games
		2c	3c		5c gym

Critical skills	Thinking Skills
problem solving	observing
decision making	classifying
critical thinking	prediction
creative thinking	making inferences
communication	problem solving
organisation	drawing conclusions
management	
leadership	

In the Dark

In the dark

Previous experience in the Foundation Stage

Most children are fascinated by dark places, and while they were in the Foundation Stage they will have:

* made dens with a variety of materials in free play both indoors and outside;
* explored concepts of light and dark through stories such as:
  * Can't you Sleep Little Bear?
  * The Bear Under the Stairs
  * The Park in the Dark
  * Funnybones
  * The Tunnel
  * A Dark Tale
* They may also have:
  * experimented with OHPs and light boxes
  * made shadows with bodies and puppets
  * played in sensory rooms and sensory toys.

Pause for thought

In the early stages of working with these materials it is crucial to continue to observe the children. Only by doing this can you set developmentally appropriate challenges and provocations. The ideas listed here are offered as suggestions; the most exciting challenges will arise from children's own interests and motivations, which will only become apparent as you spend time with them, watching and joining them in their play. As you do this, you will be moving between the three interconnecting roles of observer, co-player, extender described below, and will be able to decide what you need to do next to take the learning forward.

The responsive adult (see page 5)

In three interconnecting roles, the responsive adult will be:

observer

* observing
* listening
* interpreting

co-player

* modelling
* playing alongside
* offering suggestions
* responding sensitively
* initiating with care!

extender

* discussing ideas
* sharing thinking
* modelling new skills
* asking open questions
* being an informed extender
* instigating ideas & thoughts
* supporting children as they make links in learning
* making possibilities evident
* introducing new ideas and resources
* offering challenges and provocations

Offering challenges and provocations - some ideas:

Children need to have continuing experience of dark paces, so they can get used to different light levels, and imagine dark situations.

? Choose some stories about the dark and dark places so the children can incorporate these in their role play.

? Find some dark places for story times and role play. Black out the windows of part of your room, a shed outside, or use blankets to make a dark space under a table.

? Use puppets and small world figures with fabrics and supports to retell stories about the dark.

? Find some torches and use them to light your stories and plays.

? Make some shadow puppets for a shadow puppet show of a familiar story. Use an overhead projector to project your puppets onto a screen.

? Use a spotlight to project your own shadow onto a sheet or screen.

? Explore using coloured gels on a light box or OHP to make coloured backgrounds for your stories and shows.

? Pretend you are:
* in a wood at night
* in a cave or tunnel
* in a haunted house
* in a lift
* in an attic, loft or tower.

Now work together to make up stories about:
* why you are there
* how you got there
* what happens to you
* how the story ends.

Ready for more?

ﾟ Research dark places on the Internet, and use what you find to help you in your story telling, or make a book about dark places for other children to read.

ﾟ Record some of your stories and tell them to your friends in a dark story-telling corner.

ﾟ Find some torches and make up codes, signals and secret messages with your friends.

ﾟ Make a dark corner or place in your classroom or outside, and try some of these ideas:

   * leave messages for children or adults in the dark place
   * leave objects hidden there so your friends can use them in stories
   * play games with torches
   * take flash photos
   * make sound effect tapes
   * read or tell spooky stories.

ﾟ Make up a story about a creature or person who visits the dark place in the night, when no-one is there. What do they do? What happens?

ﾟ Google some images of dark places. Use these to make games, stories and books.

ﾟ Investigate shadows. Use torches, lights and sunlight to make, measure and draw round shadows. Watch what shadows do as the sun moves in the sky.

Materials, equipment suppliers, websites, books and other references

Suppliers: The recent improvements in production of light toys and solar lighting will make resourcing for these activities both easier and cheaper. You could try:

* petrol station bargains in solar lighting and torches;
* bargain and 'pound' shops;
* DIY stores for Christmas lights, indoor and outdoor;
* parks, events and shows for hand held lights;
* festival times and concerts;
* resources for children with special needs.

www.spacekraft.co.uk has an amazing range of lights and lighting effects at reasonable prices.

www.glow-kids-light-sticks.com has a range of glowsticks and bracelets, and www.glowsticks.co.uk have emergency sticks and other lights. For solar lights, try www.coolglowythings.com and look for a sunjar and for little video clips of some of the lights and how they work. www.TheGlowCompany.co.uk also have a huge range of glowing in the dark objects to look at.

Home stores (such as IKEA, ILVA, BHS etc) or garden centres (Homebase, B&Q etc) will also have a range of lights, solar lighting, lights specially for children, night lights and safety lights. Try **Google Images**: 'torch' 'solar light' 'glow in the dark' 'glow in the dark paint'.

Make sure you have plenty of **dark fabric** to make tents and dens for experimenting with lights.

Some **books**:

The Owl Who Was Afraid of the Dark; Jill Tomlinson; Egmont Books

How Do Bats See in the Dark? About Night Creatures; Melvin Berger; Scholastic

It Was a Dark and Stormy Night; **Burglar Bill** and **Funnybones**; all by Allan Ahlberg; Puffin

Owl Babies; Martin Waddell; Walker Books

Day Light, Night Light; Franklyn M Branley; HarperCollins

100 Things to Spot in the Night Sky; Philip Clarke; Usborne

Why Animals Live in Caves; Valerie Weber; Weekly Reader

Caves; Ellen Niz; Capstone Press

Potential NC KS1 Curriculum Coverage through the provocations suggested for in the dark

Full version of KS1 PoS on pages 69-74
Photocopiable version on page 8

Literacy

	Lit 1 speak	Lit 2 listen	Lit 3 group	Lit 4 drama	Lit 5 word	Lit 6 spell	Lit 7 text1	Lit 8 text2	Lit 9 text3	Lit10 text4	Lit11 sentence	Lit12 presentation
	1.1	2.1	3.1	4.1	5.1	6.1	7.1	8.1	9.1	10.1	11.1	12.1
	1.2	2.2	3.2	4.2	5.2	6.2	7.2	8.2	9.2	10.2	11.2	12.2

Numeracy

	Num 1 U&A	Num 2 count	Num 3 number	Num 4 calculate	Num 5 shape	Num 6 measure	Num 7 data
	1.1	2.1	3.1	4.1	5.1	6.1	7.1
	1.2	2.2	3.2	4.2	5.2	6.2	7.2

Science

	SC1 Enquiry			SC2 Life processes					SC3 Materials		SC4 Phys processes		
	Sc1.1	Sc1.2	Sc1.3	Sc2.1	Sc2.2	Sc2.3	Sc2.4	Sc2.5	Sc3.1	Sc3.2	Sc4.1	Sc4.2	Sc4.3
	1.1a	1.2a	1.3a	2.1a	2.2a	2.3a	2.4a	2.5a	3.1a	3.2a	4.1a	4.2a	4.3a
	1.1b	1.2b	1.3b	2.1b	2.2b	2.3b	2.4b	2.5b	3.1b	3.2b	4.1b	4.2b	4.3b
	1.1c	1.2c	1.3c	2.1c	2.2c	2.3c		2.5c	3.1c		4.1c	4.2c	4.3c
	1.1d				2.2d				3.1d				4.3d
					2.2e								
					2.2f								
					2.2g								

ICT

	ICT 1 finding out		ICT 2 ideas	ICT 3 reviewing	ICT 4 breadth
	1.1a	1.2a	2a	3a	4a
	1.1b	1.2b	2b	3b	4b
	1.1c	1.2c	2c	3c	4c
		1.2d			

D&T

	D&T 1 developing	D&T 2 tool use	D&T 3 evaluating	D&T 4 materials	D&T 5 breadth
	1a	2a	3a	4a	5a
	1b	2b	3b	4b	5b
	1c	2c			5c
	1d	2d			
	1e	2e			

History

	H1 chronology	H2 events, people	H3 interpret	H4 enquire	H5 org & comm	H6 breadth
	1a	2a	3a	4a	5a	6a
	1b	2b		4b		6b
						6c
						6d

Geography

	G1.1 & G1.2 enquiry		G2 places	G3 processes	G4 environment	G5 breadth
	1.1a	1.2a	2a	3a	4a	5a
	1.1b	1.2b	2b	3b	4b	5b
	1.1c	1.2c	2c			5c
	1.1d	1.2d	2d			5d
			2e			

Music

	M1 performing	M2 composing	M3 appraising	M4 listening	M5 breadth
	1a	2a	3a	4a	5a
	1b	2b	3b	4b	5b
	1c			4c	5c
					5d

PHSE & C

	PSHEC1 conf & resp	PSHEC2 citizenship	PSHEC3 health	PSHEC4 relationships
	1a	2a	3a	4a
	1b	2b	3b	4b
	1c	2c	3c	4c
	1d	2d	3d	4d
	1e	2e	3e	4e
		2f	3f	
		2g	3g	
		2h		

Art & Design

	A&D1 ideas	A&D2 making	A&D3 evaluating	A&D4 materials	A&D5 breadth
	1a	2a	3a	4a	5a
	1b	2b	3b	4b	5b
		2c		4c	5c
					5d

PE

	PE1 devel skills	PE2 apply skills	PE3 evaluate	PE4 fitness	PE5 breadth
	1a	2a	3a	4a	5a dance
	1b	2b	3b	4b	5b games
		2c	3c		5c gym

Critical skills	Thinking Skills
problem solving	observing
decision making	classifying
critical thinking	prediction
creative thinking	making inferences
communication	problem solving
organisation	drawing conclusions
management	
leadership	

Topic Collections

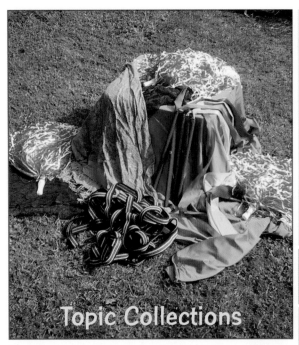

Topic Collections

Previous experience in the Foundation Stage

Throughout the Early Years Foundation Stage, children may have been offered topic related role play collections. These may have been related to:

* particular occupations;
* the seasons;
* work on a sense of time, or a sense of place;
* stories or story themes;
* walks, visits and outings;
* books, both fiction and non fiction;
* unusual events, visitors, concerts, plays or other happenings.

Pause for thought

In the early stages of working with these materials it is crucial to continue to observe the children. Only by doing this can you set developmentally appropriate challenges and provocations. The ideas listed here are offered as suggestions; the most exciting challenges will arise from children's own interests and motivations, which will only become apparent as you spend time with them, watching and joining them in their play. As you do this, you will be moving between the three interconnecting roles of observer, co-player, extender described below, and will be able to decide what you need to do next to take the learning forward.

The responsive adult (see page 5)

In three interconnecting roles, the responsive adult will be:

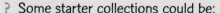

* observing
* listening
* interpreting

observer

* **modelling**
* **playing alongside**
* **offering suggestions**
* **responding sensitively**
* **initiating with care!**

co-player

* discussing ideas
* sharing thinking
* modelling new skills
* asking open questions
* being an informed extender
* instigating ideas & thoughts
* supporting children as they make links in learning
* making possibilities evident
* introducing new ideas and resources
* offering challenges and provocations

extender

Offering challenges and provocations - some ideas:

NOTE: Themed collection in bags, boxes or baskets can help children to understand and play out themes and topics where subjects are combined. They can use the collections to practice the vocabulary, knowledge and skills associated with the topic.

? Some starter collections could be:
  * a bag for a doctor, nurse or ambulance driver as part of a topic on emergency workers;
  * a picnic basket with a different cultural context (chopsticks, Asian metal dishes, clothing from a different culture) can support a PSHEC topic;
  * a collection of holiday articles in a small suitcase can stimulate understanding of a summer or holiday theme;
  * a collection of items for 'The Bear Hunt' will help the children to revisit and retell the story.

? Think about a story you have heard in the last two weeks. Now collect some objects to make a story bag. Now retell the story with your friends, using the props in the story bag.?

? Can you make a basket for a window cleaner? What would the window cleaner need?

? Can you make a prop box for:
  * a play about the seaside ?
  * a story in a Victorian house?
  * a ghost story?
  * an adventure in Africa?

? Find a box or bag and collect the things you would need to go bug hunting. Now test your collection by going on a bug hunt. Did you put the right things in?

? Draw the things you might need to make a play about one of these:
  * 'Suddenly we were in the time of the dinosaurs.'
  * 'We discovered a magical land.'
  * 'Our adventure under the sea.'
  * 'Our prize was a trip in outer space.'

Ready for more?

- Use Google images or draw some pictures to make a pictorial topic collection. Choose a topic, make the pictures, you need people as well as objects. Laminate them if you can, and put them in a pack. Deal the cards to your friends and then start a story. The first person turns over their first card and says the first sentence of the story. The next person turns over a card and says something about the object or character, and so on.

- Find a bag with a drawstring. Put some objects that go together in the bag and use the bag to make a game by feeling in the bag and saying what you think you can feel. You could make bags about:
  - the seaside
  - a farm
  - a hospital
  - a toyshop
  - the Olympics
  - your favourite sport or pop musician.

- Look on Google Images for 'story sacks', and click through to some of the websites to see what is in the sacks you can buy. You could also try the website www.storysack.com Use the information you collect to make a book all about story sacks. You could add photos of some of the things and a list of everything you could put in. Make sure you have the books in your school.

Materials, equipment suppliers, websites, books and other references

Suppliers and sources:

Topic collections can evolve over time, so keep your eyes open for likely objects to go in topic collection bags and boxes:

- objects and artefact from junk and charity shops - shoes, ornaments, crockery, pictures, photos, books;
- holiday souvenirs, brochures and postcards for history and geography collections ;
- cheap props to help with occupations - buckets, scrapers, bags, brushes, shirts to make overalls and white coats;
- props for favourite stories;
- themed fabrics to suit particular topics.

Use Google Images for pictures - just put your topic title in Google Images - for example: 'beetles' 'minibeast' (where you can click through to making minibeast traps 'cave' 'seasons' 'Africa' 'weather'.

You can also use Google Web to find topic information, www.bbc.co.uk/schools has special pages of information on Victorians and other times; www.victorians.asp-host.co.uk has 'A day in the life of' and other Victorian information.

Some books and stories:

The Olympics; Inventions; Castles; Pirates & many more topic titles in the Hot Topics Series; Peter Riley; Scholastic
Make-believe: Games & Activities for Imaginative Play; D & J Singer; American Psychological Association
Water; Castles; Fiona MacDonald; Franklin Watts
Castles (one in a series of Craft Topics); Rachel Wright; Franklin Watts
Animals in Art; Shapes in Art; Numbers in Art; Colours in Art; Lucy Micklethwaite; HarperCollins
Usborne Book of Dressing Up; Chris Caudron; Usborne
Super-simple Creative Costumes: Sue Astroth; C & T Publishing
Minibeasts; Growing; People Who help Us; Scholastic
Minibeasts, Colours, My School Day; A&C Black
Raintree Perspectives: Travel Through Time Series: Cycle Power etc; Raintree
Trains, Boats, On the Road etc; A&C Black

Curriculum coverage grid overleaf

Potential NC KS1 Curriculum Coverage through the provocations suggested for topic collections

Full version of KS1 PoS on pages 69-74
Photocopiable version on page 8

Literacy

	Lit 1 speak	Lit 2 listen	Lit 3 group	Lit 4 drama	Lit 5 word	Lit 6 spell	Lit 7 text1	Lit 8 text2	Lit 9 text3	Lit10 text4	Lit11 sentence	Lit12 presentation
Literacy	1.1	2.1	3.1	4.1	5.1	6.1	7.1	8.1	9.1	10.1	11.1	12.1
	1.2	2.2	3.2	4.2	5.2	6.2	7.2	8.2	9.2	10.2	11.2	12.2

Numeracy

	Num 1 U&A	Num 2 count	Num 3 number	Num 4 calculate	Num 5 shape	Num 6 measure	Num 7 data
Numeracy	1.1	2.1	3.1	4.1	5.1	6.1	7.1
	1.2	2.2	3.2	4.2	5.2	6.2	7.2

Science

	SC1 Enquiry			SC2 Life processes					SC3 Materials		SC4 Phys processes		
	Sc1.1	Sc1.2	Sc1.3	Sc2.1	Sc2.2	Sc2.3	Sc2.4	Sc2.5	Sc3.1	Sc3.2	Sc4.1	Sc4.2	Sc4.3
Science	1.1a	1.2a	1.3a	2.1a	2.2a	2.3a	2.4a	2.5a	3.1a	3.2a	4.1a	4.2a	4.3a
	1.1b	1.2b	1.3b	2.1b	2.2b	2.3b	2.4b	2.5b	3.1b	3.2b	4.1b	4.2b	4.3b
	1.1c	1.2c	1.3c	2.1c	2.2c	2.3c		2.5c	3.1c		4.1c	4.2c	4.3c
	1.1d				2.2d				3.1d				4.3d
					2.2e								
					2.2f								
					2.2g								

ICT

	ICT 1 finding out	ICT 2 ideas	ICT 3 reviewing	ICT 4 breadth
ICT	1.1a 1.2a	2a	3a	4a
	1.1b 1.2b	2b	3b	4b
	1.1c 1.2c	2c	3c	4c
	1.2d			

D&T

	D&T 1 developing	D&T 2 tool use	D&T 3 evaluating	D&T 4 materials	D&T 5 breadth
D&T	1a	2a	3a	4a	5a
	1b	2b	3b	4b	5b
	1c	2c			5c
	1d	2d			
	1e	2e			

History

	H1 chronology	H2 events, people	H3 interpret	H4 enquire	H5 org & comm	H6 breadth
History	1a	2a	3a	4a	5a	6a
	1b	2b		4b		6b
						6c
						6d

Geography

	G1.1 & G1.2 enquiry		G2 places	G3 processes	G4 environment	G5 breadth
Geography	1.1a	1.2a	2a	3a	4a	5a
	1.1b	1.2b	2b	3b	4b	5b
	1.1c	1.2c	2c			5c
	1.1d	1.2d	2d			5d
			2e			

Music

	M1 performing	M2 composing	M3 appraising	M4 listening	M5 breadth
Music	1a	2a	3a	4a	5a
	1b	2b	3b	4b	5b
	1c			4c	5c
					5d

PHSE & C

	PSHEC1 conf & resp	PSHEC2 citizenship	PSHEC3 health	PSHEC4 relationships
PHSE & C	1a	2a	3a	4a
	1b	2b	3b	4b
	1c	2c	3c	4c
	1d	2d	3d	4d
	1e	2e	3e	4e
		2f	3f	
		2g	3g	
		2h		

Art & Design

	A&D1 ideas	A&D2 making	A&D3 evaluating	A&D4 materials	A&D5 breadth
Art & Design	1a	2a	3a	4a	5a
	1b	2b	3b	4b	5b
		2c		4c	5c
					5d

PE

	PE1 devel skills	PE2 apply skills	PE3 evaluate	PE4 fitness	PE5 breadth
PE	1a	2a	3a	4a	5a dance
	1b	2b	3b	4b	5b games
		2c	3c		5c gym

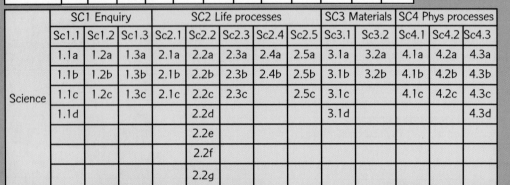

Critical skills	Thinking Skills
problem solving	observing
decision making	classifying
critical thinking	prediction
creative thinking	making inferences
communication	problem solving
organisation	drawing conclusions
management	
leadership	

Dolls and Soft Toys

Dolls and Soft Toys

Previous experience in the Foundation Stage

Children may have already had experience of using dolls and soft toys in creative and role play, indoors and outside:

* in domestic and 'home corner' play;
* for making up and retelling stories;
* in playing out their own experiences and exploring their feelings and those of others;
* in singing games and chants;
* as companions in all sorts of play;
* as an 'audience' for stories, in games and other play situations;
* to represent real or imaginary characters;
* to practice dressing and undressing, improving fine motor skills.

Pause for thought

In the early stages of working with these materials it is crucial to continue to observe the children. Only by doing this can you set developmentally appropriate challenges and provocations. The ideas listed here are offered as suggestions; the most exciting challenges will arise from children's own interests and motivations, which will only become apparent as you spend time with them, watching and joining them in their play. As you do this, you will be moving between the three interconnecting roles of observer, co-player, extender described below, and will be able to decide what you need to do next to take the learning forward.

The responsive adult (see page 5)

In three interconnecting roles, the responsive adult will be:

observer

* observing
* listening
* interpreting

co-player

* modelling
* playing alongside
* offering suggestions
* responding sensitively
* initiating with care!

extender

* discussing ideas
* sharing thinking
* modelling new skills
* asking open questions
* being an informed extender
* instigating ideas & thoughts
* supporting children as they make links in learning
* making possibilities evident
* introducing new ideas and resources
* offering challenges and provocations

Offering challenges and provocations - some ideas:

Continue to provide a wide range of dolls, soft toys and puppets for children in key Stage 1 - both boys and girls still need opportunities to externalise their thoughts and play them out through these objects. Children may also continue to need the comfort of soft toys as companions, so try to provide some toys with appeal to boys as well as girls - monkeys, wild animals, dinosaurs, dogs, Action Man toys will all have appeal for boys.

? Find a soft toy that you like and a cardboard box. Now make a home for the soft toy, using natural and recycled materials and scraps of fabric.

? Work in a group. Each one chooses a toy - an animal, a teddy bear, a doll or another sort of toy. Now decide what you are going to make for your toy - you could make hats, waterproof clothing, shoes, or sports clothes. Take photos of your toys in their clothes and make a display or book using your photos and the toys.

? Find a friend and a soft toy, action figure or doll. Sit somewhere quiet and make up a story where the toy is the hero. Now draw some pictures of the story.

? Find a camera. Now take the camera and a doll, soft toy or action figure outside. Find some adventurous places to put the character you have chosen. Take photos of the character in the adventurous place. Download the photos and make them into a story or powerpoint presentation. Add a title and some story sentences and show your story to your friends.

? Collect a basket of dolls and soft toys and hide them in the outdoor area. See how long it takes a friend to find all the toys. You could give them some clues.

? Look on the internet for soft toy manufacturers and download some pictures. Make these into a catalogue and invent a new name for each toy.

Ready for more?

- Look at some soft toy manufacturers on the internet. Work with some friends to invent some new toys. They could be:
  - action figures
  - soft toys for babies
  - story book characters
  - animal characters

  Draw your new toys, label the drawings so the manufacturer knows what each part of the drawing is. Now think of a name and write a description of what your new toy is like and what it does. Get an adult to help you choose a manufacturer and send your new idea to them. Maybe they will make it!

- Use the internet to find out about Persona Dolls. Look on Google Images first, then click through to some of the websites. Try http://dolls.nunodoll.com for some simple dolls you can make yourself, including a bat, a snake, a vampire, a kitten. Or www.starwars.com/kids/activity/crafts for instructions on making a Star Wars Yoda doll. Could you make one of these?

- Put 'peg dolls' in Google Images, and use some of the ideas to make your own peg dolls decorated with fabric, felt pen, sequins etc. You could use your peg doll to make a story or a puppet show.

- Work with some friends and a basket of soft toys or action figures. Choose a toy each and make up a character for them. Now work together to make up a story using all your characters.

Materials, equipment suppliers, websites, books and other references

Resources:

Dolls and soft toys are easy to find, often you just need to ask parents to negotiate with their children on giving up one each. Charity shops are another good source. Wherever they come from, soft toys and dolls should be washed or sponged thoroughly before the children use them, and it is wise to go through the collection regularly, discarding any that have become old or worn. Try to make your collection as wide as possible so it appeals to all children. Include:

- dolls of all sorts, sizes and ethnic backgrounds;
- adventure dolls, such as Action Man and Superhero figures;
- popular themed dolls such as Barbie, Bratz;
- small sets such as Polly Pocket and Sylvanian Families;
- soft toy animals and other creatures
- and of course, plenty of materials for making their own dolls!

Google images for ideas: 'character names' 'soft toy' 'doll' 'superhero figure' 'dolls house' and **Google web search** for information on dolls www.persona-doll-training.org has persona dolls, or try barbie.everythinggirl.com or www.americangirl.com for information on collector dolls. www.bbc.co.uk has instructions for making Worry Dolls. www.artistshelpingchildren.org will lead you to lots of doll making projects for boys and girls. www.museumeducation.bedford.gov.uk has a sheet on making peg dolls.

Some Books:
William's Doll; Charlotte Zolotow; Picture Lions
Elizabeti's Doll; Stephanie Bodeen; Lee and Low
The Little Girl and the Tiny Doll; Edward Ardizzone; Puffin
The Wise Doll (a scary fairy story); Hiawyn Oram; Andersen Press
The Doll's House: Rumer Godden; Macmillan
Feltcraft: Making Dolls, Gifts and Toys: Petra Berger; Floris Books
Toymaking with Children: Freya Jaffke; Floris Books
Puppet Planet: The Most Amazing Puppet-Making Book in the Universe!; John Kennedy; North Light Books
Make Your Own Teddy Bears and Bear Clothes: Jodie Davies; Williamson
Making Dolls: Sunnhild Reinckens; Floris Books

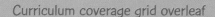

Curriculum coverage grid overleaf

Potential NC KS1 Curriculum Coverage through the provocations suggested for dolls and soft toys

Literacy

	Lit 1 speak	Lit 2 listen	Lit 3 group	Lit 4 drama	Lit 5 word	Lit 6 spell	Lit 7 text1	Lit 8 text2	Lit 9 text3	Lit10 text4	Lit11 sentence	Lit12 presentation
Literacy	1.1	2.1	3.1	4.1	5.1	6.1	7.1	8.1	9.1	10.1	11.1	12.1
	1.2	2.2	3.2	4.2	5.2	6.2	7.2	8.2	9.2	10.2	11.2	12.2

Numeracy

	Num 1 U&A	Num 2 count	Num 3 number	Num 4 calculate	Num 5 shape	Num 6 measure	Num 7 data
Numeracy	1.1	2.1	3.1	4.1	5.1	6.1	7.1
	1.2	2.2	3.2	4.2	5.2	6.2	7.2

Science

	SC1 Enquiry			SC2 Life processes					SC3 Materials		SC4 Phys processes		
	Sc1.1	Sc1.2	Sc1.3	Sc2.1	Sc2.2	Sc2.3	Sc2.4	Sc2.5	Sc3.1	Sc3.2	Sc4.1	Sc4.2	Sc4.3
Science	1.1a	1.2a	1.3a	2.1a	2.2a	2.3a	2.4a	2.5a	3.1a	3.2a	4.1a	4.2a	4.3a
	1.1b	1.2b	1.3b	2.1b	2.2b	2.3b	2.4b	2.5b	3.1b	3.2b	4.1b	4.2b	4.3b
	1.1c	1.2c	1.3c	2.1c	2.2c	2.3c		2.5c	3.1c		4.1c	4.2c	4.3c
	1.1d				2.2d				3.1d				4.3d
					2.2e								
					2.2f								
					2.2g								

ICT

	ICT 1 finding out		ICT 2 ideas	ICT 3 reviewing	ICT 4 breadth
ICT	1.1a	1.2a	2a	3a	4a
	1.1b	1.2b	2b	3b	4b
	1.1c	1.2c	2c	3c	4c
		1.2d			

Full version of KS1 PoS on pages 69-74
Photocopiable version on page 8

D&T

	D&T 1 developing	D&T 2 tool use	D&T 3 evaluating	D&T 4 materials	D&T 5 breadth
D&T	1a	2a	3a	4a	5a
	1b	2b	3b	4b	5b
	1c	2c			5c
	1d	2d			
	1e	2e			

History

	H1 chronology	H2 events, people	H3 interpret	H4 enquire	H5 org & comm	H6 breadth
History	1a	2a	3a	4a	5a	6a
	1b	2b		4b		6b
						6c
						6d

Geography

	G1.1 & G1.2 enquiry		G2 places	G3 processes	G4 environment	G5 breadth
Geography	1.1a	1.2a	2a	3a	4a	5a
	1.1b	1.2b	2b	3b	4b	5b
	1.1c	1.2c	2c			5c
	1.1d	1.2d	2d			5d
			2e			

Music

	M1 performing	M2 composing	M3 appraising	M4 listening	M5 breadth
Music	1a	2a	3a	4a	5a
	1b	2b	3b	4b	5b
	1c			4c	5c
					5d

PHSE & C

	PSHEC1 conf & resp	PSHEC2 citizenship	PSHEC3 health	PSHEC4 relationships
PHSE & C	1a	2a	3a	4a
	1b	2b	3b	4b
	1c	2c	3c	4c
	1d	2d	3d	4d
	1e	2e	3e	4e
		2f	3f	
		2g	3g	
		2h		

Art & Design

	A&D1 ideas	A&D2 making	A&D3 evaluating	A&D4 materials	A&D5 breadth
Art & Design	1a	2a	3a	4a	5a
	1b	2b	3b	4b	5b
		2c		4c	5c
					5d

PE

	PE1 devel skills	PE2 apply skills	PE3 evaluate	PE4 fitness	PE5 breadth
PE	1a	2a	3a	4a	5a dance
	1b	2b	3b	4b	5b games
		2c	3c		5c gym

Critical skills	Thinking Skills
problem solving	observing
decision making	classifying
critical thinking	prediction
creative thinking	making inferences
communication	problem solving
organisation	drawing conclusions
management	
leadership	

Playboards and Performance Areas

Playboards

Previous experience in the Foundation Stage

There will be very few children who will not, at some time in the Early Years foundation Stage, have role-played 'We're Going on a Bear Hunt' outside. They may also have:

* built houses for the Three Pigs;
* made a beanstalk for Jack to climb;
* played out Red Riding Hood's journey to Grandmother's house;
* been the Three Bears, walking through the forest;
* planned a trip to the Moon like the little bear in 'Whatever Next?';
* been transformed into a Superhero story.

The challenge for KS1 teachers is to:

* support children in expanding the challenge and complexity of their role play stories;
* identify new stories for telling out of doors.

Pause for thought

In the early stages of working with these materials it is crucial to continue to observe the children. Only by doing this can you set developmentally appropriate challenges and provocations. The ideas listed here are offered as suggestions; the most exciting challenges will arise from children's own interests and motivations, which will only become apparent as you spend time with them, watching and joining them in their play. As you do this, you will be moving between the three interconnecting roles of observer, co-player, extender described below, and will be able to decide what you need to do next to take the learning forward.

The responsive adult (see page 5)

In three interconnecting roles, the responsive adult will be:

* observing
* listening
* interpreting

* **modelling**
* **playing alongside**
* **offering suggestions**
* **responding sensitively**
* **initiating with care!**

* discussing ideas
* sharing thinking
* modelling new skills
* asking open questions
* being an informed extender
* instigating ideas & thoughts
* supporting children as they make links in learning
* making possibilities evident
* introducing new ideas and resources
* offering challenges and provocations

Offering challenges and provocations - some ideas:

Encourage children to innovate and invent new versions of well known stories - for example:

? Can you invent a new 'Bear Hunt' story - about a Lion Hunt, a Dragon Hunt, a Dinosaur Hunt, a Butterfly Hunt?

? Someone else is in the Three Bears' House. Who might it be? What will happen next?

? The Superheroes are planning a concert for the children in the hospital. What happens when they all show off their powers?

? Can you make some props and costumes for your story? Use recycled materials and see what you can do.

? Make some scenery for your story from shower curtains and big boxes.

? Now photograph or video your story and make a computer presentation or a photo story book. Or you could laminate the photos and make them into an outdoor wall story mounted on a wall.

? Create a performance area where you can act out your story with or without an audience.

? Plan and build an outside den or area specially for stories. How many people can fit in your story space?

? Design and build some spaces for stories outside, where you and your friends can go to read or write stories out of doors.
  * How will you make it comfortable?
  * How will you keep it warm and dry?
  * Who will choose and look after the books?
  * What will you provide for children who want to write or draw their own stories?

Ready for more?

- Can you make a collection of stories about pirates? Now can you make a place outside where you can play these stories? Can you make a boat?
- Can you make an outside listening area where children can go to listen to stories on CD or tape?
- Prop boxes help you to tell stories. Can you make a 'prop box' for one of your favourite stories, such as 'The Bear Hunt', 'Cinderella' or 'Finding Nemo'?
- Have a 'Story of the week'. Make an outdoor prop box for the story.
- Find some stories that you can tell in a Builder's Tray or a big seed tray of compost, using small world people and animals. Photograph or film your stories and write your own story.
- Look for some stories about eggs. Do some nest building outside as you retell the story.
- Can you find stories about monsters, or robots, or scarecrows, or castles. Design scenery for retelling them out of doors.
- Recreate some stories about growing things and nature, and make these out of doors in trays and boxes.
- Find a way of making an island or a forest outside. Use this as the basis for telling stories.
- Work in groups to produce a concert for outdoor performance. Choose a theme such as Traditional Stories, Fantasy, Animal Stories, Adventure Islands.

Materials, equipment suppliers, websites, books and other references

Some ideas for **resources and equipment**:
Playboards and performance areas. Making a space indoors or outside, where children can make and perform plays is a simple way to focus the activity while giving it status. The area doesn't have to be big, and it's a good idea to keep it flexible, with baskets of props and resources for the children to choose from. Try:

- a basket of fabrics (drapes and lengths of material) with pegs and other fastenings, wigs, hats, belts and other props;
- backpacks of story based materials - the children could collect these, or suggest items to add, stories to include etc;
- a basket of musical instruments and other sound makers;
- masks of various sorts and styles;
- a tape recorder or CD player for music.

Google 'performance areas' to get links to websites with broochures and pictures of stages and performance areas such as 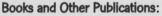 www.upstagesupplies.co.uk. www.kids-space.org has a simple playwriting game. www.openstages.co.uk for some good models of stages. **Google Images** 'outdoor performance area' 'children's theatre' 'theatre by children' 'stage' 'outdoor stage'.

Books and Other Publications:
101 Drama Games for Children, and **101 More Drama Games for Children**; Paul Rooyackers; Hunter House
Children Engaging with Drama; a downloadable version of the National Theatre report on their work with primary schools (website-archive2.nt-online.org)
Making Make-believe: Fun Props, Costumes and Creative Play Ideas; MaryAnn F. Kohl; Gryphon House
Pirates and Other Adventures (Role play); Jo Boulton; David Fulton
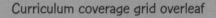 www.cornertolearn.co.uk is the site for Neil Griffiths' story sacks and performance boxes

Of course, any story, TV programme, topic or theme, or real-life incident that the children enjoy exploring can be turned into a performance.

Curriculum coverage grid overleaf

Potential NC KS1 Curriculum Coverage through the provocations suggested for playboards and performance

Full version of KS1 PoS on pages 69-74
Photocopiable version on page 8

Literacy

	Lit 1 speak	Lit 2 listen	Lit 3 group	Lit 4 drama	Lit 5 word	Lit 6 spell	Lit 7 text1	Lit 8 text2	Lit 9 text3	Lit10 text4	Lit11 sentence	Lit12 presentation
	1.1	2.1	3.1	4.1	5.1	6.1	7.1	8.1	9.1	10.1	11.1	12.1
	1.2	2.2	3.2	4.2	5.2	6.2	7.2	8.2	9.2	10.2	11.2	12.2

Numeracy

	Num 1 U&A	Num 2 count	Num 3 number	Num 4 calculate	Num 5 shape	Num 6 measure	Num 7 data
	1.1	2.1	3.1	4.1	5.1	6.1	7.1
	1.2	2.2	3.2	4.2	5.2	6.2	7.2

Science

	SC1 Enquiry			SC2 Life processes					SC3 Materials		SC4 Phys processes		
	Sc1.1	Sc1.2	Sc1.3	Sc2.1	Sc2.2	Sc2.3	Sc2.4	Sc2.5	Sc3.1	Sc3.2	Sc4.1	Sc4.2	Sc4.3
	1.1a	1.2a	1.3a	2.1a	2.2a	2.3a	2.4a	2.5a	3.1a	3.2a	4.1a	4.2a	4.3a
	1.1b	1.2b	1.3b	2.1b	2.2b	2.3b	2.4b	2.5b	3.1b	3.2b	4.1b	4.2b	4.3b
	1.1c	1.2c	1.3c	2.1c	2.2c	2.3c		2.5c	3.1c		4.1c	4.2c	4.3c
	1.1d				2.2d				3.1d				4.3d
					2.2e								
					2.2f								
					2.2g								

ICT

	ICT 1 finding out		ICT 2 ideas	ICT 3 reviewing	ICT 4 breadth
	1.1a	1.2a	2a	3a	4a
	1.1b	1.2b	2b	3b	4b
	1.1c	1.2c	2c	3c	4c
		1.2d			

History

	H1 chronology	H2 events, people	H3 interpret	H4 enquire	H5 org & comm	H6 breadth
	1a	2a	3a	4a	5a	6a
	1b	2b		4b		6b
						6c
						6d

D&T

	D&T 1 developing	D&T 2 tool use	D&T 3 evaluating	D&T 4 materials	D&T 5 breadth
	1a	2a	3a	4a	5a
	1b	2b	3b	4b	5b
	1c	2c			5c
	1d	2d			
	1e	2e			

Geography

	G1.1 & G1.2 enquiry		G2 places	G3 processes	G4 environment	G5 breadth
	1.1a	1.2a	2a	3a	4a	5a
	1.1b	1.2b	2b	3b	4b	5b
	1.1c	1.2c	2c			5c
	1.1d	1.2d	2d			5d
			2e			

Music

	M1 performing	M2 composing	M3 appraising	M4 listening	M5 breadth
	1a	2a	3a	4a	5a
	1b	2b	3b	4b	5b
	1c			4c	5c
					5d

PHSE & C

	PSHEC1 conf & resp	PSHEC2 citizenship	PSHEC3 health	PSHEC4 relationships
	1a	2a	3a	4a
	1b	2b	3b	4b
	1c	2c	3c	4c
	1d	2d	3d	4d
	1e	2e	3e	4e
		2f	3f	
		2g	3g	
		2h		

Art & Design

	A&D1 ideas	A&D2 making	A&D3 evaluating	A&D4 materials	A&D5 breadth
	1a	2a	3a	4a	5a
	1b	2b	3b	4b	5b
		2c		4c	5c
					5d

PE

	PE1 devel skills	PE2 apply skills	PE3 evaluate	PE4 fitness	PE5 breadth
	1a	2a	3a	4a	5a dance
	1b	2b	3b	4b	5b games
		2c	3c		5c gym

Critical skills	Thinking Skills
problem solving	observing
decision making	classifying
critical thinking	prediction
creative thinking	making inferences
communication	problem solving
organisation	drawing conclusions
management	
leadership	

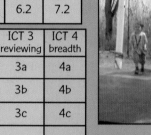

64

Do it Yourself

Do it Yourself

Previous experience in the Foundation Stage

During their time in the Foundation Stage, children will have become involved in DIY role play influenced by stories and TV programmes such as Bob the Builder. They may also have:

* worked with woodwork tools sucha s hammers, saws, screwdrivers etc. in woodworking areas;
* worked with real construction materials such as bricks, wood, gravel, sand and other substances, using barrows etc;
* observed and helped with DIY projects at home and in their early years setting;
* role-played being builders, decorators and other craftpeople when playing in construction areas both indoors and outside, in both adult and child initiated activities.

Pause for thought

In the early stages of working with these materials it is crucial to continue to observe the children. Only by doing this can you set developmentally appropriate challenges and provocations. The ideas listed here are offered as suggestions; the most exciting challenges will arise from children's own interests and motivations, which will only become apparent as you spend time with them, watching and joining them in their play. As you do this, you will be moving between the three interconnecting roles of observer, co-player, extender described below, and will be able to decide what you need to do next to take the learning forward.

The responsive adult (see page 5)

In three interconnecting roles, the responsive adult will be:

* observing
* listening
* interpreting

* modelling
* playing alongside
* offering suggestions
* responding sensitively
* initiating with care!

* discussing ideas
* sharing thinking
* modelling new skills
* asking open questions
* being an informed extender
* instigating ideas & thoughts
* supporting children as they make links in learning
* making possibilities evident
* introducing new ideas and resources
* offering challenges and provocations

Offering challenges and Provocations - some ideas:

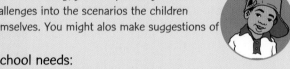

Once the children have had opportunities to explore the materials you are offering, you will probably be able to intrduce challenges into the scenarios the children develop themselves. You might alos make suggestions of your own.

? The school needs:
  * a new shed for storing toys;
  * a hutch for rabbits or a guinea pig;
  * some shelves for new books;
  * someone to repair the wheeled toys.

The children could talk about or make a plan for:
  * who will work on the team, ot do which job;
  * how to make some posters to advertise their services;
  * work out how much to charge and how much the materials will be;
  * list the materials they will need and jobs to be done.

? You or other staff could:
  * write letters to the children requesting a range of services from tidying up and sweeping the paths to building simple structures;
  * send a range of materials to be measured and catalogued;
  * request designs and suggestions for the new work that needs doing;
  * take some of the children to a DIY store or builder's yard to buy the materials you need.

? You can get 'toy' tool sets from many suppliers and toy shops. These give children a feel of the role play, without the need for close supervision. However, you may like to offer them some real bricks and wooden planks to experiment with, as they learn about making stable structures. Wheelbarrows, tool boxes and tool belts will make the role play more realistic.

Ready for more?

- You may decide to provide real, child-sized tools for the children to use. These will be much more rewarding, but need supervision.
How can the children find out where to get the tools, how much they will cost, what they need for the jobs they are going to do? Use catalogues and the internet to find the information, then the children can work to a budget and make a shopping list.

- Set up a builder's office and a building site outside. You could include:
  - a computer keyboard
  - clipboards and pens
  - tool boxes and belts
  - mobile phones and phone books
  - hard hats and reflective waistcoats
  - wheelbarrows, shovels etc
  - plans and diagrams
  - catalogues of furniture, plumbing, building supplies.

- See if you can find a local building site to look at. Health and Safety rules will probably prevent you from going inside, but you might be able to get a builder to come and talk to the children about what they do and the tools they use.

- Visit a DIY superstore (if you let them know you are coming, you might gt someone to talk toi the children). Look at all the tools and equipment and take some photos to use for displays and stories.

Materials, equipment suppliers, websites, books and other references

Some ideas for resources and equipment:

Building, making, carrying and mixing are all activities that fascinate children, and doing these in role makes them even better. When encouraged, girls enjoy this play as much as boys do. Collect some of these:
- child sized or toy tools, tool boxes and tool belts;
- buckets, wheelbarrows, boots and hard hats;
- planks, tyres, fabrics and cable reels;
- boxes, bags and baskets;
- recycled materials such as guttering and drainpipes;
- ropes, pegs; cable clips;
- clipboards, pens, a phone and a computer keyboard;
- a teapot and mugs for making tea, and a tent or shelter to use as a tea tent.

www.leevalley.com have tools for children, fun.familyeducation.com/crafts have a list of tools for a children's toolbox, www.kidscanmakeit.com takes you to a site with lots of projects for children to make. Try www.taunton.com and click through to 'techniques' to find help with woodwork at school. Websites for builders' tools and equipment are easy to find through Google, and there are some good images of tools in Google Images 'tools' (where you can find a poster of old fashioned tools) 'builder's tools' 'toolbox' 'bricks' 'kids tools' and get a copy of the ASE booklet 'Be Safe' from www.ase.org.uk a very useful booklet on safety in technology and science in primary schools.

Books and Publications:

Tools We Use: Builders: Dana Meachen Rau; Benchmark Books
Jobs People Do: A Day in the Life of a Builder: Linda Hayward; Dorling Kindersley
Easy Carpentry Projects for Children: Jerome Leavitt;
Harvey the Carpenter and Harvey the Painter: Lars Klinting; Kingfisher
Builder for a Day: Dawn Sirett; Dorling Kindersley
Big Builders: Susan Korman; Inchworm
Miss Brick the Builder's Baby: Allan Ahlberg; Puffin
Easy Carpentry Projects for Children: Jerome Leavitt; Dover
Carpentry for Children: Lester Walker; Overlook Press
Woodworking for Kids: Kevin McGuire; Sterling Juvenile

Curriculum coverage grid overleaf

Potential NC KS1 Curriculum Coverage through the provocations suggested for 'do it yourself'

Literacy	Lit 1 speak	Lit 2 listen	Lit 3 group	Lit 4 drama	Lit 5 word	Lit 6 spell	Lit 7 text1	Lit 8 text2	Lit 9 text3	Lit10 text4	Lit11 sentence	Lit12 presentation
	1.1	2.1	3.1	4.1	5.1	6.1	7.1	8.1	9.1	10.1	11.1	12.1
	1.2	2.2	3.2	4.2	5.2	6.2	7.2	8.2	9.2	10.2	11.2	12.2

Numeracy	Num 1 U&A	Num 2 count	Num 3 number	Num 4 calculate	Num 5 shape	Num 6 measure	Num 7 data
	1.1	2.1	3.1	4.1	5.1	6.1	7.1
	1.2	2.2	3.2	4.2	5.2	6.2	7.2

Full version of KS1 PoS on pages 69-74
Photocopiable version on page 8

Science	SC1 Enquiry			SC2 Life processes					SC3 Materials		SC4 Phys processes		
	Sc1.1	Sc1.2	Sc1.3	Sc2.1	Sc2.2	Sc2.3	Sc2.4	Sc2.5	Sc3.1	Sc3.2	Sc4.1	Sc4.2	Sc4.3
	1.1a	1.2a	1.3a	2.1a	2.2a	2.3a	2.4a	2.5a	3.1a	3.2a	4.1a	4.2a	4.3a
	1.1b	1.2b	1.3b	2.1b	2.2b	2.3b	2.4b	2.5b	3.1b	3.2b	4.1b	4.2b	4.3b
	1.1c	1.2c	1.3c	2.1c	2.2c	2.3c		2.5c	3.1c		4.1c	4.2c	4.3c
	1.1d				2.2d				3.1d				4.3d
					2.2e								
					2.2f								
					2.2g								

ICT	ICT 1 finding out		ICT 2 ideas	ICT 3 reviewing	ICT 4 breadth
	1.1a	1.2a	2a	3a	4a
	1.1b	1.2b	2b	3b	4b
	1.1c	1.2c	2c	3c	4c
		1.2d			

D&T	D&T 1 developing	D&T 2 tool use	D&T 3 evaluating	D&T 4 materials	D&T 5 breadth
	1a	2a	3a	4a	5a
	1b	2b	3b	4b	5b
	1c	2c			5c
	1d	2d			
	1e	2e			

History	H1 chronology	H2 events, people	H3 interpret	H4 enquire	H5 org & comm	H6 breadth
	1a	2a	3a	4a	5a	6a
	1b	2b		4b		6b
						6c
						6d

Geography	G1.1 & G1.2 enquiry		G2 places	G3 processes	G4 environment	G5 breadth
	1.1a	1.2a	2a	3a	4a	5a
	1.1b	1.2b	2b	3b	4b	5b
	1.1c	1.2c	2c			5c
	1.1d	1.2d	2d			5d
			2e			

Music	M1 performing	M2 composing	M3 appraising	M4 listening	M5 breadth
	1a	2a	3a	4a	5a
	1b	2b	3b	4b	5b
	1c			4c	5c
					5d

PHSE & C	PSHEC1 conf & resp	PSHEC2 citizenship	PSHEC3 health	PSHEC4 relationships
	1a	2a	3a	4a
	1b	2b	3b	4b
	1c	2c	3c	4c
	1d	2d	3d	4d
	1e	2e	3e	4e
		2f	3f	
		2g	3g	
		2h		

Art & Design	A&D1 ideas	A&D2 making	A&D3 evaluating	A&D4 materials	A&D5 breadth
	1a	2a	3a	4a	5a
	1b	2b	3b	4b	5b
		2c		4c	5c
					5d

PE	PE1 devel skills	PE2 apply skills	PE3 evaluate	PE4 fitness	PE5 breadth
	1a	2a	3a	4a	5a dance
	1b	2b	3b	4b	5b games
		2c	3c		5c gym

Critical skills	Thinking Skills
problem solving	observing
decision making	classifying
critical thinking	prediction
creative thinking	making inferences
communication	problem solving
organisation	drawing conclusions
management	
leadership	

The following pages contain the detail for the curriculum key which appears at the end of each section of the book. The appendix consists of the following:

1. Short-hand versions of the QCA/DfES Programme of Study for Key Stage 1 in:

Science
Information & Communication Technology
Design and Technology
History
Geography
Music
Art and Design
Physical Education

2. The suggested programme of study for Personal, Social and Health Education and Citizenship (PSHE & C)

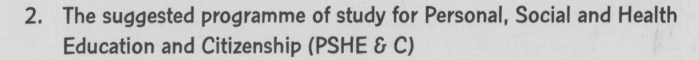

3. The elements of the guidance for learning and teaching of Literacy and Numeracy in Years 1 and 2 (from the Primary Framework for literacy and mathematics; DfES/SureStart; Sept 2006; Ref: 02011-2006BOK-EN)

Literacy 1 speaking	Literacy 2 listening & responding	Literacy 3 group discussion & interaction	Literacy 4 drama	Literacy 5 word recognition, coding & decoding	Literacy 6 word structure & spelling	Literacy 7 understanding & interpreting texts	Literacy 8 engaging & responding to text	Literacy 9 creating and shaping texts	Literacy 10 text structure & organisation	Literacy 11 sentence structure & punctuation	Literacy 12 presentation
Year 1 Tell stories and describe incidents from their own experience in an audible voice Retell stories, ordering events using story language Interpret a text by reading aloud with some variety in pace and emphasis Experiment with & build new stores of words to communicate in different contexts	**Year 1** Listen with sustained concentration, building new stores of words in different contexts Listen to and follow instructions accurately, asking for help and clarification if necessary Listen to tapes or video and express views about how a story or information has been presented	**Year 1** Take turns to speak, listen to others' suggestions and talk about what they are going to do Ask and answer questions, make relevant contributions, offer suggestions and take turns Explain their views to others in a small group, decide how to report the group's views to the class	**Year 1** Explore familiar themes and characters through improvisation and role-play Act out their own and well-known stories, using voices for characters Discuss why they like a performance	**Year 1** Recognise & use alternative ways of pronouncing the graphemes already taught, for example, that the grapheme 'g' is pronounced differently in 'get' and 'gem'; the grapheme 'ow' is pronounced differently in 'how' & 'show' Recognise and use alternative ways of spelling the phonemes already taught, for example 'ae' ' can be spelt with 'ai', 'ay' or 'a-e'; begin to know which words contain which spelling alternatives Identify the constituent parts of two-syllable and three-syllable words to support the application of phonic knowledge and skills Recognise automatically an increasing number of familiar high frequency words Apply phonic knowledge & skills as the prime approach to reading & spelling unfamiliar words that are not completely decodable Read more challenging texts which can be decoded using their acquired phonic knowledge & skills; automatic recognition of high frequency words Read and spell phonically decodable two-syllable and three-syllable words	**Year 1** Spell new words using phonics as the prime approach Segment sounds into their constituent phonemes in order to spell them correctly Children move from spelling simple CVC words to longer words that include common diagraphs & adjacent consonants such as 'brush', 'crunch' Recognise & use alternative ways of spelling the graphemes already taught, for example that the /ae/ sound can be spelt with 'ai', 'ay' or 'a-e'; that the /ee/ sound can also be spelt as 'ea' and 'e'; & begin to know which words contain which spelling alternatives Use knowledge of common inflections in spelling, such as plurals, -ly, -er Read & spell phonically decodable 2- & 3 syllable words	**Year 1** Identify the main events and characters in stories, and find specific information in simple texts Use syntax and context when reading for meaning Make predictions showing an understanding of ideas, events and characters Recognise the main elements that shape different texts Explore the effect of patterns of language & repeated words & phrases	**Year 1** Select books for personal reading and give reasons for choices Visualise and comment on events, characters and ideas, making imaginative links to their own experiences Distinguish fiction and non-fiction texts and the different purposes for reading them	**Year 1** Independently choose what to write about, plan and follow it through Use key features of narrative in their own writing Convey information and ideas in simple non-narrative forms Find and use new and interesting words and phrases, including story language Create short simple texts on paper and on screen that combine words with images (and sounds)	**Year 1** Write chronological and non-chronological texts using simple structures Group written sentences together in chunks of meaning or subject	**Year 1** Compose and write simple sentences independently to communicate meaning Use capital letters and full stops when punctuating simple sentences	**Year 1** Write most letters, correctly formed and orientated, using a comfortable and efficient pencil grip Write with spaces between words accurately Use the space bar and keyboard to type their name & simple texts
Year 2 Speak with clarity and use appropriate intonation when reading and reciting texts Tell real and imagined stories using the conventions of familiar story language Explain ideas and processes using imaginative and adventurous vocabulary and non-verbal gestures to support communication	**Year 2** Listen to others in class, ask relevant questions and follow instructions Listen to talk by an adult, remember some specific points and identify what they have learned Respond to presentations by describing characters, repeating some highlight and commenting constructively	**Year 2** Ensure that everyone contributes, allocate tasks, and consider alternatives and reach agreement Work effectively in groups by ensuring that each group member takes a turn challenging, supporting and moving on Listen to each other's views and preferences, agree the next steps to take and identify contributions by each group member	**Year 2** Adopt appropriate roles in small or large groups and consider alternative courses of action Present part of traditional stories, their own stories or work drawn from different parts of the curriculum for members of their own class Consider how mood and atmosphere are created in live or recorded performance	**Year 2** Read independently and with increasing fluency longer and less familiar texts Spell with increasing accuracy and confidence, drawing on word recognition and knowledge of word structure, and spelling patterns Know how to tackle unfamiliar words that are not completely decodable Read and spell less common alternative graphemes including trigraphs Read high and medium frequency words independently and automatically	**Year 2** Spell with increasing accuracy and confidence, drawing on word recognition and knowledge of word structure, and spelling patterns including common inflections and use of double letters Read and spell less common alternative graphemes including trigraphs Understanding and interpreting texts	**Year 2** Draw together ideas & information from across a whole text, using simple signposts in the text Give reasons why things happen or characters change Explain organisational features of texts, including alphabetical order, layout, diagrams etc Use syntax & context to build their store of vocabulary when reading Explore how particular words are used, including words & expressions with similar meanings	**Year 2** Read whole books on their own, choosing and justifying selections Engage with books through exploring and enacting interpretations Explain their reactions to texts, commenting on important aspects	**Year 2** Draw on knowledge and experience of texts in deciding and planning what & how to write Sustain form in narrative, including use of person & time Maintain consistency in non-narrative, including purpose & tense Make adventurous word and language choices appropriate to the style and purpose of the text Select from different presentational features to suit particular writing purposes on paper & on screen	**Year 2** Use planning to establish clear sections for writing Use appropriate language to make sections hang together	**Year 2** Write simple and compound sentences and begin to use subordination in relation to time and reason Compose sentences using tense consistently (present & past) Use question marks, and use commas to separate items in a list	**Year 2** Write legibly, using upper and lower case letters appropriately within words, and observing correct spacing within and between words Form and use the four basic handwriting joins Word process short narrative and non-narrative texts

NC KS1 Programme of Study - Literacy

(revised Framework objectives)

Numeracy 1 using and applying mathematics	Numeracy 2 counting & understanding number	Numeracy 3 knowing & using number facts	Numeracy 4 calculating	Numeracy 5 understanding shape	Numeracy 6 measuring	Numeracy 7 handling data
Year 1 **Solve problems** involving counting, adding, subtracting, doubling or halving in the context of numbers, measures or money, for example to 'pay' & 'give change' **Describe a puzzle or problem** using numbers, practical materials & diagrams; use these to solve the problem & set the solution in the original context **Answer a question** by selecting and using suitable equipment, and sorting information, shapes or objects; display results using tables and pictures **Describe simple patterns** and relationships involving numbers or shapes; decide whether examples satisfy given conditions **Describe ways of solving puzzles** and problems, explaining choices and decisions orally or using pictures	**Year 1** **Count reliably** at least 20 objects, recognising that when rearranged the number of objects stays the same; estimate a number of objects that can be checked by counting **Compare and order numbers,** using the related vocabulary; use the equals (=) sign **Read and write numerals from 0 to 20,** then beyond; use knowledge of place value to position these numbers on a number track and number line **Say the number that is 1 more or less than any given number,** & 10 more or less for multiples of 10 **Use the vocabulary of halves and quarters** in context	**Year 1** **Derive and recall all pairs of numbers with a total of 10** and addition facts for totals to at least 5; work out the corresponding subtraction facts **Count on or back in ones, twos, fives and tens** and use this knowledge to derive the multiples of 2, 5 and 10 to the tenth multiple **Recall the doubles of all numbers to at least 10**	**Year 1** **Relate addition to counting on;** recognise that addition can be done in any order; use practical and informal written methods to support the addition of a one-digit number or a multiple of 10 to a one-digit or two- digit number **Understand subtraction as 'take away'** and find a 'difference' by counting up; use practical and informal written methods to support the subtraction of a one-digit number from a one-digit or two-digit number and a multiple of 10 from a two- digit number **Use the vocabulary related to addition and subtraction and symbols** to describe and record addition and subtraction number sentences **Solve practical problems** that involve combining groups of 2, 5 or 10, or sharing into equal groups	**Year 1** **Visualise and name common 2-D shapes and 3-D solids** and describe their features; use them to make patterns, pictures & models **Identify objects that turn about a point** (e.g. scissors) or about a line (e.g. a door); recognise & make whole, half & quarter turns **Visualise & use everyday language to describe** the position of objects and direction and distance when moving them, for example when placing or moving objects on a game board	**Year 1** **Estimate, measure, weigh and compare objects,** choosing & using suitable uniform non-standard or standard units & measuring instruments (e.g. a lever balance, metre stick or measuring jug) **Use vocabulary related to time;** order days of the week & months; read the time to the hour & half hour	**Year 1** **Answer a question** by recording information in lists & tables; present outcomes using practical resources, pictures, block graphs or pictograms **Use diagrams to sort objects into groups** according to a given criterion; suggest a different criterion for grouping the same objects
Year 2 **Solve problems** involving addition, subtraction, multiplication or division in contexts of numbers, measures or pounds and pence **Identify and record the information or calculation needed to solve a puzzle or problem;** carry out the steps or calculations and check the solution in the context of the problem **Follow a line of enquiry;** answer questions by choosing and using suitable equipment and selecting, organising and presenting information in lists, tables and simple diagrams **Describe patterns and relationships** involving numbers or shapes, make predictions and test these with examples **Present solutions to puzzles and problems** in an organised way; explain decisions, methods and results in pictorial, spoken or written form, using mathematical language and number sentences	**Year 2** **Read and write two-digit and three-digit numbers in figures and words;** describe and extend number sequences and recognise odd and even numbers **Count up to 100 objects** by grouping them and counting in tens, fives or twos; explain what each digit in a two-digit number represents, including numbers where 0 is a place holder; partition two-digit numbers in different ways, including into multiples of 10 and 1 **Order two-digit numbers** and position them on a number line; use the greater than (>) and less than (<) signs **Estimate a number of objects;** round two-digit numbers to the nearest 10 **Find one half, one quarter and three quarters** of shapes and sets of objects	**Year 2** **Derive and recall all addition and subtraction facts** for each number to at least 10, all pairs with totals to 20 and all pairs of multiples of 10 with totals up to 100 **Understand that halving is the inverse of doubling** and derive and recall doubles of all numbers to 20, and the corresponding halves **Derive and recall multiplication facts for the 2, 5 and 10 times-tables** and the related division facts; recognise multiples of 2, 5 and 10 **Use knowledge of number facts and operations** to estimate and check answers to calculations	**Year 2** **Add or subtract mentally a one-digit number or a multiple of 10 to or from any two-digit number;** use practical and informal written methods to add and subtract two-digit numbers **Understand that subtraction is the inverse of addition and vice versa;** use this to derive and record related addition and subtraction number sentences **Represent repeated addition and arrays as multiplication,** and sharing and repeated subtraction (grouping) as division; use practical and informal written methods and related vocabulary to support multiplication and division, including calculations with remainders **Use the symbols +, -, ?, ÷ and = to record and interpret number sentences** involving all four operations; calculate the value of an unknown in a number sentence	**Year 2** **Visualise common 2-D shapes and 3-D solids;** identify shapes from pictures of them in different positions and orientations; sort, make and describe shapes, referring to their properties **Identify reflective symmetry in patterns and 2-D shapes** and draw lines of symmetry in shapes **Follow and give instructions** involving position, direction and movement **Recognise and use whole, half and quarter turns,** both clockwise and anticlockwise; know that a right angle represents a quarter turn	**Year 2** **Estimate, compare & measure lengths, weights and capacities,** choosing & using standard units (m, cm, kg, litre) & suitable measuring instruments **Read the numbered divisions on a scale,** and interpret the divisions between them (e.g. on a scale from 0 to 25 with intervals of 1 shown but only the divisions 0, 5, 10, 15 and 20 numbered); use a ruler to draw and measure lines to the nearest centimetre **Use units of time** (seconds, minutes, hours, days) and know the relationships between them; read the time to the quarter hour; identify time intervals, including those that cross the hour	**Year 2** **Answer a question** by collecting and recording data in lists and tables; represent the data as block graphs or pictograms to show results; use ICT to organise and present data **Use lists, tables and diagrams to sort objects;** explain choices using appropriate language, including 'not' **Programme of Study - Numeracy** **(revised Framework objectives)**

SC1 scientific enquiry			SC2 life processes & living things					SC3 materials and their properties		SC4 physical processes		
Sc1.1 planning	Sc1.2 ideas & evidence; collecting evidence	Sc1.3 comparing evidence	Sc2.1 life processes	Sc2.2 humans and other animals	Sc2.3 green plants	Sc2.4 variation and classification	Sc2.5 living things in their environment	Sc3.1 grouping materials	Sc3.2 changing materials	Sc4.1 electricity	Sc4.2 forces and motion	Sc4.3 light and sound
1.1a ask questions 'How?', 'Why?', 'What if?') and decide how they might find answers to them	1.2a follow simple instructions to control the risks to themselves and to others	1.3a make simple comparisons (eg, hand span, shoe size) and identify simple patterns or associations, and try to explain it, drawing on their knowledge and understanding	2.1a differences between things that are living and things that have never been alive	2.2a recognise and compare the main external parts of the bodies of humans and other animals	2.3a recognise that plants need light and water to grow	2.4a recognise similarities and differences between themselves and others, and to treat others with sensitivity	2.5a find out about the different kinds of plants and animals in the local environment	3.1a use their senses to explore and recognise the similarities and differences between materials	3.2a find out how the shapes of objects made from some materials can be changes by some processes, including squashing, bending, twisting & stretching	4.1a about everyday appliances that use electricity	4.2a find out about, & describe the movement of, familiar things (e.g. cars going faster, slowing down, changing direction)	4.3a identify different light sources, including the Sun
1.1b use first-hand experience & simple information sources to answer questions	1.2b explore, using the senses of sight, hearing, smell, touch & taste as appropriate, & make & record observations & measurements	1.3b compare what happened with what they expected would happen, and try to explain it. Drawing on their knowledge and understanding	2.1b that animals, including humans, move, feed, grow, use their senses and reproduce	2.2b that humans and other animals need food and water to stay alive	2.3b to recognise and name the leaf, flowers, stem and root of flowering plants	2.4b group living things according to observable similarities and differences	2.5b identify similarities & differences between local environments & ways in which these affect animals & plants that are found there	3.1b sort objects into groups on the basis of their properties texture, float, hardness, transparency & whether they are magnetic or non-magnetic)	3.2b explore & describe the way some everyday materials) for example water, chocolate, bread, clay, change when they are heated or cooled	4.1b simple series circuits involving batteries, wires, bulbs and other components - eg buzzers	4.2b that both pushes and pulls are examples of forces	4.3b that darkness is the absence of light
1.1c think about what might happen before deciding what to do	1.2c communicate what happened in a variety of ways, including using ICT	1.3c review their work and explain what they did to others	2.1c relate life processes to animals and plants found in the local environment	2.2c that taking exercise and eating the right types and amounts of food help humans to keep healthy	2.3c that seeds grow into flowering plants		2.5c care for the environment	3.1c recognise and name common types of material & recognise that some of them are found naturally		4.1c how a switch can be used to break a circuit	4.2c to recognise that when things speed up, slow down or change direction, there is a cause	4.3c that there are many kinds of sound and sources of sound
1.1d Recognise when a test or comparison is unfair				2.2d about the role of drugs as medicines				3.1d find out about the uses of a variety of materials & how these are chosen for specific uses on the basis of their simple properties				4.3d that sounds travel away from sources, getting fainter as they do so, and that they are heard

2.2e how to treat animals with care and sensitivity

2.2f that humans and other animals can produce offspring and that these offspring grow into adults

2.2g about the senses that enable humans and other animals to be aware of the world around them

NC KS1 Programme of Study for Key Stage 1- Science

NC KS1 Programme of Study - ICT

ICT 1 — 1.1 finding things out / 1.2 developing ideas and making things happen		ICT 2 — exchanging and sharing information	ICT 3 — reviewing, modifying & evaluating work as it progresses	ICT 4 — breadth of study
1.1a gather information from a variety of sources	**1.2a** use text, tables, images & sound to develop their ideas	**2a** share their ideas by presenting information in a variety of forms	**3a** review what they have done to help them develop their ideas	**4a** work with a range of information to investigate the ways it can be presented
1.1b enter & store information in a variety of forms	**1.2b** select from and add to information they have	**2b** present their completed work effectively	**3b** describe the effects of their actions	**4b** exploring a variety of ICT tools
1.1c retrieve information that has been stored	**1.2c** plan & give instructions to make things happen		**3c** talk about what they might change in future work	**4c** talk about the uses of ICT inside and outside school
	1.2d try things out & explore what happens in real & imaginary instructions			

NC KS1 Programme of Study - History

H1 chronological understanding	H2 K & U of events, people & changes	H3 historical interpretation	H4 historical enquiry	H5 organisation & communication	H6 breadth of study
1a place events and objects in chronological order	**2a** recognise why people did things, why events happened and what happened as a result	**3a** identify different ways in which the past is represented	**4a** find out about the past from a range of sources of information	**5a** select from their knowledge of history and communicate it in a variety of ways	**6a** changes in their own lives and the way of life of their family or others around them
1b use common words and phrases relating to the passing of time (for example, before, after, a long time ago, past	**2b** identify differences between ways of life at different times		**4b** ask and answer questions about the past		**6b** the way of life of people in the more distant past who lived in the local area or elsewhere in Britain
					6c the lives of significant men, women and children
					6d past events from the history of Britain and the wider world

NC KS1 Programme of Study - D&T

D&T 1 developing planning & communicating ideas	D&T 2 working with tools, equipment, materials	D&T 3 evaluating processes & products	D&T 4 k & u of materials & components	D&T 5 breadth of study
1a generate ideas	**2a** explore sensory qualities of materials	**3a** talk about their ideas	**4a** working characteristics of materials	**5a** focused practical tasks
1b develop ideas	**2b** measure, mark out, cut and shape	**3b** identify improvements	**4b** how mechanisms can be used	**5b** design & make assignments
1c talk about their ideas	**2c** assemble, join & combine materials			**5c** investigate & evaluate products
1d plan what to do next	**2d** use simple finishing techniques			
1e communicate ideas	**2e** follow safe procedures			

NC KS1 Programme of Study - Geography

G1.1 & G1.2 geographical and enquiry skills		G2 knowledge & understanding of places	G3 knowledge & understanding of patterns & processes	G4 knowledge & understanding of environment	G5 breadth of study
1.1a ask geographical questions	**1.2a** use geographical vocabulary	**2a** identify & describe what places are like	**3a** make observations about where things are located	**4a** recognise changes in the environment	**5a** the locality of the school
1.1b observe and record	**1.2b** use fieldwork skills	**2b** identify and describe what places are	**3b** recognise changes in physical & human features	**4b** recognise how the environment may be improved & sustained	**5b** a contrasting locality in the UK or overseas
1.1c express their own views about people, places & environments	**1.2c** use globes, maps & plans at a range of scales	**2c** recognise how places become they way they are & how they are changing			**5c** study at a local scale
1.1d communicate in different ways	**1.2d** use secondary sources of information	**2d** recognise how places compare with other places			**5d** carry out fieldwork investigations outside the classroom
		2e recognise how places are linked to other places in the world			

Programme of Study for Key Stage 1- Art & Design

A&D1 exploring & developing ideas	A&D2 investigating & making art, craft and design	A&D3 evaluating & developing work	A&D4 k & u of materials & components	A&D5 breadth of study
1a record from first hand observation, experience & imagination	2a investigate the possibilities of materials and processes	3a review what they and others have done	4a visual and tactile elements	5a exploring a range of starting points
1b ask and answer questions about the starting points for their work	2b try out tools & techniques & apply these	3b identify what they might change	4b materials & processes used in making art, craft & design	5b working on their own, and collaborating with others
	2c represent observations, ideas and feelings		4c differences & similarities in the work of artists, craftspeople & designers	5c using a range of materials and processes
				5d investigating different kinds of art, craft & design

Programme of Study for Key Stage 1- Music

M1 performing skills	M2 composing skills	M3 responding & reviewing (appraising skills)	M4 responding & reviewing (listening skills)	M5 breadth of study
1a use their voices expressively by singing songs, chants, rhymes	2a create musical patterns	3a explore and express their ideas and feelings about music	4a listen with concentration & internalise & recall sounds	5a a range of musical activities
1b play tuned & untuned instruments	2b explore, choose & organise sounds & musical ideas	3b make improvements to their own work	4b how combined musical elements can be organised	5b responding to a range of starting points
1c rehearse and perform with others			4c how sounds can be made in different ways	5c working on their own, in groups & as a class
				5d a range of live and recorded music

Programme of Study for Key Stage 1- PE

PE1 acquiring and developing skills	PE2 selecting and applying skills, tactics and compositional ideas	PE3 evaluating and improving performance	PE4 knowledge and understanding of fitness and health	PE5 breadth of study
1a explore basic skills, actions and ideas with increasing understanding	2a explore how to choose & apply skills and actions in sequence & in combination	3a describe what they have done	4a how important it is to be active	5a dance
1b remember & repeat simple skills & actions with increasing control	2b vary the way they perform skills by using simple tactics and movement phrases	3b observe, describe & copy what others have done	4b recognise & describe how their bodies feel during different activities	5b games
	2c apply rules and conventions for different activities	3c use what they have learnt to improve the quality and control of their work		5c gymnastics

Programme of Study for Key Stage 1- PSHE

PSHEC1 developing confidence & responsibility & making the most of their abilities	PSHEC2 preparing to play an active role as citizens	PSHEC3 developing a healthier lifestyle	PSHEC4 developing good relationships & respecting differences
1a recognise their likes & dislikes, what is fair & unfair, what is right & wrong	2a take part in discussions with one other person and the whole class	3a make simple choices that improve their health & wellbeing	4a recognise how their behaviour affects other people
1b share their opinions on things that matter to them and their views	2b take part in a simple debate about topical issues	3b maintain personal hygiene	4b listen to other people and play and work co-operatively
1c recognise, name and deal with their feelings in a positive way	2c recognise choices they make, & the difference between right & wrong	3c how some diseases spread and can be controlled	4c identify and respect differences and similarities between people
1d think about themselves, learn from their experiences & recognise what they are good at	2d realise that people and other living things have needs, & that they have responsibilities to meet them	3d about the process of growing from young to old & how people's needs change	4d that family and friends should care for each other
1e how to set simple goals	2e that they belong to various groups & communities, such as a family	3e the names of the main parts of the body	4e that there are different types of teasing & bullying, that bullying is wrong
	2f what improves & harms their local, natural & built environments	3f that household products & medicines, can be harmful	
	2g contribute to the life of the class and school	3g rules for, and ways of, keeping safe, basic road safety	
	2h realise that money comes from different sources		

Credits and references

Web sites included in this book (in alphabetical order):

www.5aday.nhs.uk nhs site for the national fruit scheme

www.activityvillage.co.uk for instructions and templates for making your own bunting;

www.artistshelpingchildren.org instructions for making and using all sorts of boxes, doll making for boys and girls

www.ascoeducational.co.uk for empathy dolls, small world play, play mats and vehicles

www.ase.org.uk a very useful booklet (Be Safe) on safety in technology and science in primary schools.

www.amazon.co.uk for cheap plastic food and other role play equipment

www.americangirl.com for information on collector dolls

www.argos.co.uk for cheap tea-sets

www.barbie.everythinggirl.com

www.britishcouncil.org/kids-stories-treasure-map for a treasure map and story

www.auntannie.com/puppets.html is an electronic book of crafts including puppets

www.bbc.co.uk/schools has special pages of information on Victorians and other historical times

www.victorians.asp-host.co.uk has 'A day in the life of' and other Victorian information and instructions for making Worry Dolls

www.christchurchcofeschool.co.uk to see their Year 1 projects

www.communityplaythings.co.uk for role play furniture

www.coolglowythings.com and look for a Sunjar and for little video clips of some of the lights and how they work.

www.TheGlowCompany.co.uk also have a huge range of 'glow in the dark' objects to look at.

www.cornertolearn.co.uk is the site for Neil Griffiths' story sacks and performance boards

www.cottonbunting.co.uk a site with skull and crossbone bunting and lots of other designs

www.crawler.com - then 'treasure map for kids' will get you to lots of downloadable treasure maps and ideas including a treasure collection set in jelly

www.dh.gov.uk/en/Publicationsandstatistics/Publications/PublicationsPolicyAndGuidance/DH Free fruit scheme and where you will find a leaflet to download

www.dh.gov.uk/en/Publichealth/Healthimprovement/FiveADay/FiveADaygeneralinformation

http://dharmashop.com shows lots of Tibetan prayer flags

www.domesticproduct.co.uk for a prizewinning design for a willow playhouse

www.earlyvision.co.uk role play dvd for everyday situations such as the airport, garage, hotel

www.earlyyearsresources.co.uk have play food, shopping baskets and furniture

www.easy-child-crafts.com/salt-dough-recipes

www.ecocentric.co.uk - sell a model castle and other toys made from recycled cardboard

www.ed-solutionsdirect.coms.co.uk for role play furniture

www.enchantedlearning.com/crafts/puppets for ideas and instructions

http://flags.midlandimports.com sell flags of all nations

fun.familyeducation.com/crafts have a list of tools for a children's toolbox

www.gigglemoose.com/salt_dough_recipe for salt dough recipes

www.glow-kids-light-sticks.com has a range of glowsticks and bracelets www.glowsticks.co.uk have emergency sticks and other lights

www.holyspiritinteractive.net/kids/artsncrafts - click through to making boxes for instructions on making different shapes and kinds of boxes, with templates

www.jellydeal.co.uk have some good deals on workbenches, kitchens, cash registers, and a 120 piece play food set

www.kid-at-art.com - an art site for children with an 'Imagination Factory' of ideas

www.kidscanmakeit.com takes you to a site with lots of projects for children to make

www.kids-space.org has a simple playwriting game

www.leevalley.com have tools for children

www.make-stuff.com/kids - has some great projects including a cardboard castle.

www.markfennell.com/flags has pictures of flags of all countries;

www.midpac.co.uk has a huge range of ribbon and other trimmings.

www.mindstretchers.co.uk - have den building kits, shade sails, waterproof sheets and willow structures

www.mrflag.com will make a flag to your own design;

www.museumeducation.bedford.gov.uk has a sheet on making peg dolls

www.nationalgeographic.com/pirates - also about pirates, with lots of books and other information.

www.openstages.co.uk for some good models of stages

www.persona-doll-training.org has persona dolls

www.piratesinfo.com - just about pirates!

www.portfolio-display.co.uk for lots of design ideas;

www.puppetsbypost.com for a huge selection of puppets of all sizes and types

www.savvysource.com - is an encyclopedia of craft ideas

www.spacekraft.co.uk has an amazing range of lights and lighting effects at reasonable prices.

www.standards.dfes.gov.uk/schemes2 is a government contact for a KS1 curriculum topic on moving toys

www.streetparty.org.uk for pictures of street parties;

www.taunton.com and click through to 'techniques' to find help with woodwork at school

www.terragenesis.co.uk - model castle using textured paint.

www.threebearsplaythings.co.uk sell a pack of ten fabric collection bags for £6:50 and role play fabrics, barrier tape (stripey), ribbon, play screens

www.thriftyfun.com - for ideas of making containers from all sorts of things

www.tts-group.co.uk also have a great role play cloaks set, pirate chest, role play trolley, tabards, masks, screens, backgrounds for play,

www.ukoln.ac.uk - and click through to find Treasure Island for things to make, games and challenges

www.upstagesupplies.co.uk for stages

www.vam.ac.uk is a site where you can download clips of moving toys

www.walkerbooks.co.uk have a great selection of their own books about fantasy and imagination sorted by age group and Key Stage.

http://woodentotsmk.co.uk for role play equipment and furniture

http://woodfield.ethink.org.uk/2008 (a school site) and look at their pop-up-puppets

www.worldwidesmiles.biz festivals of clowns

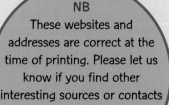

NB
These websites and addresses are correct at the time of printing. Please let us know if you find other interesting sources or contacts
sally@featherstone.uk.com.

Carrying on in Key Stage One

Other titles in this series include:

Construction

Sand

Water

Outdoor Play

Sculpting, Stuffing and Squeezing

www.acblack.com/featherstone

The EYFS – Birth to Three

Little Baby Books offer lots of ideas for working with young children, and match the original birth to three framework.

A Strong Child **A Skilful Communicator** **A Competent Learner** **A Healthy Child**

Set 1
978-1-905019-21-2

Set 2
978-1-905019-22-9

Set 3
978-1-905019-23-6

Set 4
978-1-905019-24-3

Also available with the activities grouped according to stage.

Book 1 Heads-up Lookers & Communicators (124pp)
978-1-905019-50-2

Book 2 Sitters, Standers & Explorers (156pp)
978-1-905019-51-9

Book 3 Movers, Shakers & Players (172pp)
978-1-905019-52-6

Book 4 Walkers, Talkers & Pretenders (238pp)
978-1-905019-53-3

> All the activities in these books are suitable for the EYFS. Just look for the component and age you need.

Heads-up Lookers & Communicators Stage 1: 0-8 months

Sitters, Standers & Explorers Stage 2: 8-18 months

Movers, Shakers & Players Stage 3: 18-24 months

Walkers, Talkers & Pretenders Stage 4: 24-36 months

Foundations Activity Packs

Ages 3–5

Each pack: • pbk, resources & CD £24.99 • 305 x 225 mm
• 48pp • colour photographs, black and white illustrations

These award-winning activity packs are bursting with resources – ideal for all adults working with children aged 3–5.

Written by Early Years practitioners and experts.

"Everything you need to plan, organise and lead activities on early years themes"
Montessori International

The resources in each pack include:
- 50+ easy-to-follow activities
- 14 photocopiable activity sheets
- 8 colour photocards
- CD of poems, songs and stories
- Giant themed display poster
- Planning chart

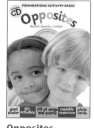

Celebrations
Kate Tucker
9780713668452

Opposites
Rachel Sparks Linfield
9780713662191

My School Day
Ann Montague-Smith
9780713661583

Minibeasts
Christine Moorcroft
9780713662184

Playsongs

Livelytime Playsongs
Sheena Roberts & Rachel Fuller
Early Years practitioner/parent resource:
- £9.99
- pbk (32pp) + CD

9780713669404

Baby's active day in songs and pictures.
A picture songbook which tells the story of a baby's day in glorious full colour and in songs with clearly described actions. Dances, peekaboo, finger and toeplays, teasers, knee bouncers and lullabies. 0–3 years

Sleepytime Playsongs
Sheena Roberts & Rachel Fuller
Early Years practitioner/parent resource:
- £9.99
- pbk (32pp) + CD

9780713669411

Baby's restful day in songs and pictures.
A picture songbook and CD which tells the story of baby's restful day in glorious full colour and in songs with clearly described actions. 0–3 years

Playsongs
Early Years/practitioner/parent resource:
- £12.99
- pbk (48pp) + CD

9780713663716

72 songs and rhymes for babies and toddlers.
The perfect musical start for the very young – fully illustrated book and CD. 0–3 years

To see our full range of books visit www.acblack.com

Continuity and progression through the EYFS

The Baby & Beyond series takes simple activities or resources and shows how they can be used with children at each of the EYFS development stages, from birth to 60+ months. Each double page spread covers one activity, so you can see the progression at a glance.

Shows how simple resources can be used by children at different ages and stages

Ideal to support progression and extend learning.

Inspiration for planning continuous provision

Messy Play	978-1-905019-58-8
The Natural World	978-1-905019-57-1
The Sensory World	978-1-905019-60-1
Sound and Music	978-1-905019-59-5
Mark Making	978-1-905019-78-6
Construction	978-1-905019-77-9
Dolls & Soft Toys	978-1-905019-80-9
Bikes, Prams, Pushchairs	978-1-905019-76-2
Role Play	978-1-906029-02-9
Finger Play & Rhymes	978-1-906029-01-2
Dens & Shelters	978-1-906029-03-6
Food	978-1-906029-04-3

To see our full range of books visit www.acblack.com